FAIR FIGHT! EVEN THE ACADEMIC PLAYING FIELD

EVERYONE'S GUIDE THROUGH MEDICAL SCHOOL, LAW SCHOOL, PROFESSIONAL SCHOOL, AND ALL HIGHER EDUCATION

HOWARD COOK

authorHOUSE

AuthorHouse™
1663 Liberty Drive
Bloomington, IN 47403
www.authorhouse.com
Phone: 833-262-8899

Published by AuthorHouse 07/13/2021

ISBN: 978-1-6655-0073-9 (sc)
ISBN: 978-1-6655-0074-6 (hc)
ISBN: 978-1-6655-0220-7 (e)

Library of Congress Control Number: 2020918923

Print information available on the last page.

DEDICATION

This book is dedicated to my Mother and Father Una Cook and Kenneth Cook, my wife Kimberly Cook, my children Candice, Jessica, Brittany, and Howie, my sister Valerie Jaques, and brother Kenneth Cook. Robbie, Aunt Saundra, Ruben, Cecilly, all of my cousins, and all of the people who helped me along the way.

The entire premise of this book is to be OVER PREPARED. OVER PREPARED, OVER PREPARED for whatever program you are going to. It does not matter if it is medical school, engineering program, law school, flight school, or the fire or police academy. Many times when people from underserved groups try to get into professional programs they are always considered to be lacking or in need of special favors to get in and get through. This is not true. It is only that they have not have the opportunity to prepare like their majority counter parts. Everyone has heard about the preparatory schools that rich kids go to like Sidwell Friends, and Georgetown Prep. It is not a coincidence that these parents with money send their kids to these affluent schools. If the kids truly take advantage of the education there then often times they will be prepared/overprepared for pre-med, pre-law, and pre-engineering programs at most universities - even the elite schools. Now public schools try to use AP or advanced placement courses to try and even the playing fields.

Affirmative action was needed during segregation because no matter how good the student was during that time they could still not be considered for entrance into programs only because of the color of their skin. It is still needed but not because blacks and people of color are not capable. Even though we all know that they are more than capable unfortunately stereotypes of minorities have perpetuated the idea that people of color or of lower socioeconomic status are of inferior intelligence. All brains are gray! (They are not inferior, and are many times superior because of the adversity (oppression and being marginalized) that they have to overcome.) Regardless of where or how they were raised.

Years ago there used to be a thing called a ringer. A ringer was considered someone who was already a professional where his competitors were amateurs. In other words, an amateur boxing competition should only have amateur boxers in it. What would happen is people who were professional boxers would enter amateur competitions and win. They were considered ringers. This continues today. There are people who are going into difficult endeavors tend to study, practice at whatever they do before they go and start that particular activity. Just like many of the Tuskegee airmen became private pilots before they went and applied to the program. Some of them were even instructor pilots before they applied. This enabled them to have the greatest chance of success when applying to the program. Much less famous my squad leader did 3 years of engineering education before entering West Point. So you want to be someone who achieves academic excellence because they've had the courses before in high school, prep school, community college, or four-year college. Even if they have taken the courses as an audit which means that you take courses for no college credit. But the key is to keep the old test and any other study material that will be beneficial, and memorize it completely to the point where you can reproduce each test without looking at it and understand why the problems are done the way they are.

This book was written to even the playing field, and to help those with the desire to obtain the ability to go to and complete the best academic programs in the country that you want to attend. It may take more work and or more resources, but it can be done. Essentially it takes learning the course work before you go to the program just as some of the Tuskegee airmen knew how to fly before they applied to the program, Just as Benjamin O Davis went to college before he attended West Point to become the first Black graduate of the US Military Academy in the 20th century. Or General Hal Moore of the First Air Cavalry fame went to George Washington University before attending West Point.

This brings me to my Black Star Man (Person) Initiative (Beat the Dean!!). At the military academies there is an honor designation among cadets. Those in the top 5% of the class are designated star men/women/people. These cadets where gold stars on their collars/lapels/pockets (not the stap stars). I would like to make Black Star Men a common sight rather than a rarity. The way to do that is to have them adequately/over prepared for entrance into the academic programs. In other words before going to the academy study electrical engineering at a community college. Most community colleges that have engineering programs, and the courses that you should include are calculus, chemistry, physics, and engineering. You will also need to take one or two English courses because you need to know how to write essays, as well express yourself. Take a foreign language that will help you to know the one you want to take. Taking these courses and learning them like the back of your hand will free up a lot of your time and thought processes, because you will not be learning for the first time. Also allowing you to get the highest grades that you can so your class rank will allow you to get the branch (assignment) you want. If you are worried about the grades hurting your GPA − − Audit the courses!! (Take the courses for no credit and save the notes and old test. Memorize them so you can reproduce them without looking at them with the understanding of how the problems are done and then retake the course for credit if you want to.) In this book we are not concerned with getting into your school of choice or medical school professional school choice, because we know with your drive and determination you will get into somewhere you want to go whether it is Harvard, Yale, University of Michigan, University of Miami, UCLA,

PCOM, Nova Southeastern University DO or MD program, Lake Erie College of Osteopathic Medicine, Ross University, or St. Georges University. Our main concern/goal is to get you in and through as well as possible with the least amount of suffering (wondering if you're going to pass rather than how high an "A" you are going to get).

MEDICAL SCHOOL

The best medical school for you to go to is the one you can graduate from!! You're not going to medical school to be a permanent medical student (in other words not finish) the goal is to graduate with your best possible grade point average, and understanding of the material so you will be able to move on to the next phase as well prepared as possible.

This is the medical school section. It does not really matter which school you go to for undergraduate as long as you are able to learn and finish there. Same thing for medical school. There are over 171 Allopathic medical schools, and 36 Osteopathic medical schools with 57 locations. There are also off shore medical schools. There are 9 schools of Podiatry, there are 23 schools of Optometry, 66 schools of dentistry in the U.S.. For the people who think that it does matter, or you don't need to be overprepared then I am not talking to them, they obviously have some advantage such as a photographic memory or are able to learn large amounts of material easily or they have taken it before in some other form - and they have their own agenda. If you want to teach at an Ivy league school well it might matter if you went to an Ivy league medical school, but like I said that is a separate agenda. Our goal is to graduate with the most knowledge about medicine so that when you attend the school of your choice you should almost be there for the doctor/diploma rubber stamp. There should be no question about finishing, only about how well. You should only be worried about how high your GPA will be, because you know the information so thoroughly that you are rubberstamping but I going to school. There was a classmate of mine named Lynn who was in ICU nurse for 10 years before she came to medical school and every test she took in the 1st and 2nd years had no lower than 98% for grade. She went on to become a plastic surgeon. This type of preparation will also allow you to enjoy your medical school experience for as much of it as can be enjoyed, because you are overprepared or super prepared for medical school.

Now usually people are in a hurry and do the minimum prep for medical school, or do just enough to get in and in many cases this causes them to suffer and worry about getting through academically. Of course, it can be done, and those of you with a photographic memory – I'm not talking to you, or those with the capacity to learn large amounts of new information easily – I'm not talking to you either. I'm talking to the normal human beings who want to do well with minimal suffering, and worry.

Medical school is the professional school that students attend to become physicians. There are several different types of physicians MDs that are allopathic physicians, DOs that are osteopathic physicians, DPM who are podiatric physicians, ODs that are optometric physicians, DC's that are chiropractic physicians, PAs that are not physicians but physician assistants, NP's that are nurse practitioners who operate, or perform as care or specialists physicians, Pharm D's who are pharmacists with a doctorate in pharmacy, PhD's, who are not physicians, but in some foreign countries this degree is required with their version of the MD. DSC's who are doctorates in science in many different subjects.

MD, allopathic physicians - - are physicians that are supposed to try to counteract symptoms of an illness originally. Now MDs and DOs consider themselves well-rounded and holistic physicians and the only real difference between the two is the fact that osteopathic manipulation is taught in the DO schools, but not taught in the MD schools. Even though some MDs choose to learn about osteopathic manipulation.

DO's, osteopathic physicians - - are physicians that are supposed to look at all aspects of the patient and their illness and treat them in a holistic and all-encompassing manner. The idea is to consider all aspects of the patient and illness. In the beginning, osteopathic physicians considered osteopathic manipulation one of their main tools for healing. Mind you that this was a time when there was very little scientific development of medication and most versions of medication were developed through trial and error. In this day and age manipulation helped with chronic ailments such as back pain and joint pain, and in some circles was considered an excellent way to try and maintain health.

DDS, DMD - - dentists are physicians that treat and do surgery on teeth. In some cases they actually helped reconstruct places of accident victims that have been disfigured. They may do this with the help of plastic surgeons, or they may actually be a dentist in a plastic surgeon themselves. That is called maxillofacial surgery.

DPMs, podiatric physicians - - are physicians who treat patients from the mid calf down. They mostly work on the foot and ankle, but they have to go to medical school that teaches them about the entire body. Just like MDs and DOs.

ODs optometric physicians - - are physicians that evaluate and treat diseases of the and also perform refractions, so that people may have classes that allow them to seek better.

DC's chiropractic physicians - - are physicians who manipulate muscle and bone to treat maladies that afflict the physical structure. In particular, the back, and their adjustments help to improve motion and comfort.

Pharm.D. pharmacist - - are professionals that take prescriptions and dispense medication so that the public can get there appropriate medication for their specific maladies.

PAs physician assistants - - are people who have trained as physician assistants, which is like a mini medical school, and many times perform same jobs as physicians do.

NP's nurse practitioners - - are nurses who have studied beyond the RN, in the BSN to get the nurse practitioner degree which is a Masters degree, and is being upgraded by the profession to be a doctorate in nursing, which is most likely another ivory tower attempt to have their degree but more difficult to obtain, at a time when nurse practitioners are most needed out in the field and not in the world of academia.

PhD's doctorate in philosophy - - are the true doctors in almost every subject matter. Many times they consider MDs and DO's and has technicians when it comes to the true understanding of biochemistry, physiology and pharmacology. PhD's can be obtained in most disciplines including English, history and other academic pursuits. Because they require a thesis (which can involve a large political process) other degrees have been created such as DSC's and EdD's.

DSC's doctorate of science - - degree was created to obtain a doctorate level degree without necessarily writing a doctorial dissertation. They can be obtained in physics and engineering, and other scientific pursuits. Even Sheldon has one in addition to his PhD.

As time has gone on they are starting to require written projects that rival doing the dissertation.

One Female physician I met had a PhD was a microbiology major in undergraduate, studied pathobiology in graduate school then went on to medical school and aced it. Then she did a residency in pathology, and this physician was one of the most knowledgeable physicians I had ever met.

Ways to become one:

There are several ways to go to medical school. There is the least expensive way, there is the traditional way, and there are many untraditional routes to medical school. But the most important way to go to medical school according to this book is to be over prepared when you get there. This can involve training in your undergraduate, or graduate school preparation before you try to enter professional school, which is to medical school.

The least expensive way - - the cheapest way to become a physician.

1. Attend community college for the first two years of your education, which could be free or nearly free of charge. 2. Earned a scholarship to the last two years of undergraduate study through Phi Theta Kappa, or some other scholarship for your academic achievement, such as Marc scholarship, (Department of Defense, Department of Energy, etc.) or from some other governmental agency. Then to add in the over prepared component you could do a biomedical Masters degree, or a Masters degree in physiology, pharmacology, microbiology, molecular biology, or pathology. These Masters degrees are usually funded (as a research assistant, or a teacher assistantship) and you can have a stipend to live on for as much as $25,000 a year. Then you will apply to medical school.

2. The least expensive way to go to medical school would be to get a full scholarship to undergraduate. This can be done in a number of ways. Good grades and SAT scores are key. Sometimes Caucasian students can obtain diversity scholarships at historically black colleges and universities (HBCU's), which would take care of the burden of the undergraduate cost for school. This can also translate to obtaining a full scholarship to the historically black colleges and universities, medical schools and law schools. This may allow you to essentially do your entire undergraduate and medical/legal education for free. A few of these schools are Meharry Medical College, Howard medical school Morehouse medical college, and for law Howard University law school, North Carolina Central University law

school, Southern law school, and Florida A&M University law school. This may also be true for pharmacy, and other professional school as well as undergrad. Look into it.

There was one physician that I knew a Caucasian female who ended up going to Howard University medical school for free. She had done a year of service in the Peace Corps previously only because she wanted to. She then attended Howard's Medical School for free even though her mother was wealthy. Her mother's situation is neither here nor there. She then went on to do her residency in surgery, and is a practicing surgeon today with no medical school monetary debt.

There are several different ways to go to medical school. The different routes are a combination of options for going into different schools to achieve your goal.:

1. You need 90 credit hours to get into most allopathic medical school programs. You need a bachelor's degree to get into the osteopathic medical school programs. You can go to community college and obtain enough credits to go to a four year college to finish the curriculum for applying to medical school. Many medical schools still only require 90 semester credit hours to get accepted. Of course your grades would have to be exceptional, along with a high MCAT (you can improve with study books, study courses, or tutors). So community college with transfer to a four year college to finish out the at least 90 credit hours to get accepted to medical school is one option. This scenario will play out like this. You graduate from high school to go to the community college and concentrate on biological courses that will prepare you for medical school including biology 1 and 2, anatomy and physiology 1 and 2, microbiology, parasitology, virology, bacteriology, histology, biochemistry 1 and 2 if at all possible. Organic chemistry is a course that is given to premed majors to weed them out and is rarely used in medical school

except for chair and boat confirmations of chemical formulas. Even if you major in physical education, kinesiology, physical therapy it would be a good idea to take these other courses so you will have seen them before you take them in medical school. You can even major in English, journalism, or history, but you will need to take the above courses to get yourself ready to get in and through as successfully as possible. You can major in anything as long as you include the courses you need!!

2. Then there is going to a 4 year college to complete a 4 year curriculum to go to medical school where you take the MCAT, and major in something that should help you to get in. If you decide not to major in any medical curriculum you could be a history or English (because plenty of people major and nonscientific majors and end up going to medical school) major but you would need to take the courses that you are going to seen in medical school not exclusively but to include : Anatomy, Physiology, Histology, Microbiology (to include parasitology, virology, and bacteriology), Neurology, pathology, and pharmacology. These are the courses that you are going to see in the first year of medical school. Although now many schools have gone to a system based approach to teaching medical school yet these approaches still require that you know the content of the courses named above. This is the most traditional path for going to medical school.

Sometimes studying genetics is helpful to some people when they're taking the embryology part of a course.

3. There are also specialized programs where you complete undergraduate and medical school together in 6 years. There are about 67 of these programs. In these programs will complete your undergraduate program in 3 years and the medical school program in 3 years. Some of the programs have you complete the undergraduate in 2 years and leave the graduate program

at 4 years length. There are many of these programs available to people who are prepared to go into them. Many times they would have had preparatory courses in high school, prep school, or their preparatory program before entering the 6 year program.

4. With time not being a factor, one of the best most prepared ways of getting into medical school is to start a Masters or PhD program in one of the concentrations like physiology, pharmacology, and pathology (biophysics, molecular biology, microbiology are some of the other concentrations). If you start the PhD and your school has an MD/PhD program you may be invited (sometimes) to do the MD program because in the 2nd year of the PhD program, you may start teaching some of the course work for the 1st year MD students, and you may be invited to join the MD program. This seems to be understated, but this is one of the most important tips for getting medical school if you feel that your record is not good enough to get into the school that you would like to go to. Getting into a PhD program in pursuing it even if you are not invited to join the MD program it will prepare you academically to complete usually any MD program that you apply to afterwards including places like Harvard, Yale, Johns Hopkins, Cornell, Stanford, Columbia University, Duke University, University of Pennsylvania, PCOM, VCOM, St. Georges University School of Medicine, or Ross University School of Medicine. Many times in medical school you will find that your classmates have Masters degrees in these disciplines and some of them already have PhD's in these areas of study giving them quite an advantage over the rest of their classmates. In one medical school one of the teachers for pharmacology joined the next year's medical school class and eventually graduated with one of the highest GPA's ever obtained at that school. He used that to get himself a ophthalmology residency at a place where no

D.O.'s had ever been accepted for ophthalmology residency. He was one of the top graduates in the history of the school.

There was one of the microbiology teachers who had a PhD in microbiology, and seemed to be angry at the medical students for being in medical school because he wanted to become a physician from what he told us. He as a PhD in microbiology could have easily gone on to any medical school program after obtaining his PhD and it easily aced it rather than being angry at the students he was teaching for the next 30 years. It is possible that his life circumstances may not have allowed for time to go onto medical school. Yet the pharmacology teacher who went on to enroll at the same medical school where he was teaching because he felt that if these medical students can do this and my knowledge and ability is greater than theirs then why shouldn't I?

Some of the newer medical school programs may also allow you to accelerate your learning process if you are someone who has a great amount of academic knowledge such as a PhD in pathology. Thereby allowing you to shorten the academic phase of medical school by one year and finish in 3 years.

5. Foreign medical schools are sometimes more flexible as to when you can start medical school. They will allow you to start in January, and sometimes in the summer depending upon the situation. Some of these schools you can do their academic program year-round which saves you time for example if you are a nontraditional student and you are married with children and trying to get through the academic portion of medical school as fast as you can so you can go on to do your clinical training back in the states near your family or in another country near your family. This is only one reason why you would like to possibly do a nontraditional program that would allow you control your time a little more. They allow admissions on what is called a rolling admission basis. For example, Ross University

school of medicine has three different start dates. They admit students in January, May, and September. This means that you are not locked into starting in August or September which is the traditional beginning of a semester year. But there are prejudices built into every system. If you graduate from an offshore medical school it will be difficult for you to get a residency in any of the surgery residencies except for OB/GYN. That is because OB/GYN is considered a primary care specialty. Specialties like urology and orthopedics you may have trouble even being considered for because you finished at an offshore medical school. This has to do with pecking order and competition for residencies/very specialized residencies that are sought after. This is because there are prejudices built into the system. There are politics involved like visiting the program directors, like cutting their grass, shining shoes, taking their kids to school, or picking up the dry cleaning – – now some of that is a bit tongue-in-cheek, but there is some truth behind it.

As previously stated in number five above, there are offshore medical schools which you can apply to also, but to date you can not use the financial aid, or scholarships that you can use for the other medical schools. Some of the schools are: Ross University and St. Georges University, and the rest are listed in the foreign medical school section. Some of the scholarships like national health service Corps scholarship, Indian health care service Corps scholarship, Hispanic health service Corps scholarship, Army health service Corps scholarship, Navy health service Corps scholarship, Air Force health service Corps scholarship cannot be used at these foreign medical schools by the time this book is being published. Yet you can do the loan repayment programs once you finish your residency if you are eligible. Remember when joining the military you should do it because you want to be in the military when you take the military scholarships. The job of the military is to fight, and you may get injured or killed doing your job.

The books to help you with the MCAT, DAT, Pharm CAT, OAT are Kaplan or Barron's books to study for the test. There are other books like Princeton review, Cliffs notes, Princeton review, or for dummies series. It just depends on which books suit you the best.

One strategy for these exams is to 1st study for the entire exam is best you can with the exam review books listed below by studying for several months and spread it out. Probably 3 to 4 months doing 10 problems a day with the answer key and the explanation of why the answers are correct. Memorize these nuggets of information as you go along. Use their note cards or make your own notecards so you know the information without having to look at it. Then once you have taken the tests if you are not satisfied with your score try studying one section of the study book more intensely than you do the other sections so you do super well on that section especially if you have an affinity for. For example if you are a biologist and you study of biology section to you is simply have it memorized and all the appropriate answers and why their right, or if you are a physicist or a chemist and you study that section until you have memorized all the answers and why they are right then take the exam again making sure that you concentrate on that section. This could significantly boost your score if you do this for one or 2 sections may be having to take the tests a total of 3 times or 2 times depending on how you work it, and thereby obtaining the score you desire.

1. Kaplan MCAT 528
2. Barron's MCAT
3. Kaplan DAT prep plus
4. Oat prep plus
5. PCAT (Barron's, Cliffs Test Prep)

The best majors to be in for medical school education are:

1. PHARMACY/PHARMACOLOGY
2. PHYSIOLOGY
3. PATHOLOGY
4. MICROBIOLOGY

The best programs to complete before you go to medical school are:

1. Pharm D
2. Physicians Assistant
3. BSN or RN.

You may ask why would you already want to be a Doctor of Pharmacy or a physician assistant before you go? Because you will walk into the school having seen most of the knowledge that is required in med school in addition to knowing it very well (like the back of your hand). This would allow you to get the highest grade that you possibly can, and match closest to the specialty/residency that you want! Many people want to get Dermatology, Ophthalmology, Orthopedic surgery, and Plastic surgery (used to need a fellowship but may be one complete program now). For those who are interested in attending Ivy League schools for medicine and are concerned that they would not be able to keep up once admitted then these suggestions should be considered. In our class we had five pharmacist, three chiropractors, one veterinarian, and one PhD in chemistry. Then we had numerous (as many as 50 people) masters degrees in physiology, pathology and microbiology, and every time we took a test the top 50 grades out of 150 people will be no lower than 98%.

There are also the Biomedical Science Masters degrees - in some places called POST BAC for post baccalaureate degree. Which are the degree programs that had my idea before I even had it. They are aimed at having you take a essentially all of the first year medical school courses before you go to the first year of medical school. In some programs you actually take your classes with the first year medical students. Then you repeat the same courses when you are in your first year of medical school. The idea is to prepare or overprepared you - make you a ringer allowing you to get hopefully the highest grades you can possibly get. Georgetown University was one of the 1st programs actually dedicated to this purpose. The POST BAC or Pre-Med. Georgetown has a program that is a Masters in physiology and many schools have this program now. Nova southeastern University college of osteopathic and allopathic medicine have a post baccalaureate program that gives excellent preparation for entering medical school. During this year you have another chance to take the MCAT and you could literally be a history English or other type of major but with this intense program you would be as good or most as good as someone who majored in physiology or pharmacology. Maybe not with the same depth of knowledge but still a good chance of doing well in your 1st year.

As Pharmacist you are very familiar with what most people go to the doctor for. When you go to the doctor you will most likely get a prescription for your particular ailment. So as a pharmacist you dispense medication and have to know all about the body and the body systems, along with receptors, and how the medications alter the body processes to make you better. In addition to knowing toxicology and how much medication is therapeutic as well as how much medication is dangerous. So you know essentially what a physician knows when it comes to taking care of patients except you don't to clinical treatments. That is not completely true anymore because pharmacists do give injections for the flu and for pneumonia.

A Physician assistant has already gone to a mini medical school and is extremely prepared for medical school. Many PA's have gone on to medical school and done very very well so if you are concerned that you will not make it into medical school or make it through medical school this might be one of the things to consider doing before you go.

Some even practice for a year or two before moving onto medical school. And if for any reason you can't go on to medical school he still get to work like a physician treat patients, and do surgery if desired. Physician assistants are more inclined to do surgery/be surgical assistance, and no's practitioners are more inclined to be primary care or floor practitioners like in a cardiac unit.

Pathology masters or undergraduate degree is all encompassing when it comes to medicine One joke is that Surgery can do everything but knows nothing, Internal medicine knows everything but does nothing, and Pathology does everything and knows everything but it is a day too late. Because with pathology you learn all of the bodies different systems including cardiovascular, pulmonary, gastrointestinal, l neurologic, integumentary, hematology and oncology. Literally all of the systems and processes in the body to include the alterations of many surgical procedures, and how the surgeries are done procedure wise, how they are supposed to correct, or alter bodily functions.

Microbiology is one field where you learn most of medicine. Parisitology, Virology, and Bacteriology include many of the illnesses that humans and other animals contract. In this field you learn how the diseases alter the human body to cause disease, and how the treatments help the body to defeat the disease. To know that you have to know how the human body is in its non diseased state. Thereby affording you a vast amount of knowledge about the human body, and almost all of the disease processes.

On the back end there are those who feel like their undergraduate career will not afford them the opportunity to get into any medical school, and they may be correct. One way to improve their record would be to add graduate work in the form of a Masters degree that concentrates on one of the fields such as pharmacy, or pharmacology physiology, pathology, microbiology. Many of these programs might offer scholarships and stipends secondary to conducting research and teaching while studying. This graduate study can include a biomedical

Masters degree which is like doing the 1st year of medical school if the medical school offers it. Many times these graduate students take classes with the actual 1st year medical students and then go on to do their 1st year the next year. Georgetown university was one of the 1st places to have a program like this but they called it a physiology Masters.

Another important way to improve your GPA is to retake the courses you did poorly in to raise the GPA. Because medical schools and professional school applications count all of the grades from every program or school you attended even if it doesn't raise the GPA that you graduate with at one particular school it will help to improve your overall GPA because the medical school application service or professional school application service will average all of the grades together.

It doesn't hurt to repeat courses especially when you gain a deeper and better knowledge of the particular course that you are taking and it is going to be needed in the professional school that you plan to attend. An extreme example of this is that one of my classmates have was literally in his 5th medical school when he came to our class. Previously he had been in 4 other medical schools and has left them for various reasons which were not revealed to us. It is very possible that he came from a medical family and plan to make it through no matter what or that he had extenuating circumstances that kept him from finishing the other 4 times, but he did graduate with us and is now a practicing physician.

Some people go on to work on a PhD degree at a university that has a medical school. Many times once you are into the 2nd year of the PhD program they may offer you the opportunity to complete a MD degree along with the PhD for free. The second-year PhD students usually end up teaching some of the medical school classes and during this time the department may offer you the opportunity to do your MD along with the PhD. Even if that doesn't not occur if you have a PhD in one of the above areas of study you will more than likely be accepted to any MD program that you apply to.

There are actual programs that combine the MD/PhD. These programs are called MD/PhD programs and usually afford the opportunity to have free or waived tuition along with a $25,000 stipend yearly until completion. The amount of funding for each individual program varies depending on the school. There are approximately 119 of these MD/PhD programs.

Books that will help you during medical school are:

1. Physiology Coloring book
2. Anatomy Coloring book
3. Cardiology Coloring book
4. Microbiology made ridiculously simple
5. Pathology made ridiculously simple
6. Physiology made ridiculously simple
7. Pharmacy made ridiculously simple
8. Super Memory Super Student by Harry Lorayne - most important book that enables you to add this method of memory to your academic arsenal. These will help if you are a visual learner like me.
9. Netters collection of medical books is also very helpful in seeing the drawings of the conditions along with the explanation that is provided. This helps especially if you are a visual learner.

Books that will help for the boards are:

1. USMLE first aid for the boards for (USMLE 1)
2. Family Practice Review by Richard Swanson - if you are someone who learns by answering questions and reading their explanations. This book helped me for parts two and three (of the licensing boards). There are at least 4 tests that are

needed once you finish medical school, and 5 if you are taking subspecialty. True the test have changed so you will have to judge for yourself what will help you the most. There are many series of books including for dummies series and made simple series that you may find helpful.

3. Once you have passed the licensing boards you will need to take your specialty and subspecialty boards, and the series of books/programs are MKSAP, and Med Study. Pass machine, and med Challenger are good courses to purchase when studying for your boards, and would probably be a good addition when you are in residency. Taking these courses throughout your residency training when doing each subject is a good idea. You would listen to the lectures for that section of the boards when you went on that particular rotation, and you would do as many of the questions along with the answer to for each section of the boards. It is not just a good idea to go over these but to literally memorize everything that is in that particular section and why the answers to their questions are correct. Then reviewed these questions and lectures as often as possible before you take your specialty board. In addition, to these programs there are tutoring services that are available. They are expensive, but if you need them they will be worth it when you pass. Many times the tutoring services are done online and cost as much as $15,000 for 40 hours of tutoring. Other tutoring courses such as Pass Machine and MedChallenger cost about $1000 apiece depending on what you buy. These programs also allow you to get CME's and keep up your continuing medical education credits on a yearly basis.

FOREIGN MEDICAL SCHOOLS

There are also many offshore medical schools that are located in the Caribbean. Some of those medical schools are as follows. There is a school of thought that considers the top 4 medical schools in this area to be the best. You would have to decide for yourself. As stated before the best medical school for you to go to is the one you can graduate from. That stuff about worrying about going to a top-ranked medical school does you no good if you're not able to complete the course of curriculum and graduate.

It seems that it does matter what law school you go to if you are trying to get in with certain firms and have certain political and financial opportunities. But with medicine if you are exceptional with what you do it doesn't matter as much where you graduate from. 2 doctors who were from my medical University made a point of memorizing every page in Harrison's internal medicine verbatim literally word for word. They were able to quote location of the information and chapter and verse in this voluminous medical resource. In addition, there was a medical school graduate from the St. Georges University medical school in Grenada named Dr. Chakuma who was one of the best doctors I ever encountered.

1. St. Georges University Medical School

2. Ross University School of Medicine: (also has a Chancellor's academic achievement award which is offered to students who maintain high standards of academic performance during undergraduate studies minimum undergraduate overall GPA of 3.8 on a 4.0 scale and minimum "old" MCAT score 28, new MCAT score of 505, must hold undergraduate degree or equivalent and award is open to incoming 1st semester and students only - award amount $24,170 which is the full cost of 1st semester tuition one time scholarship for 1st semester)
3. American University of Antigua
4. Avalon University School of Medicine
5. Trinity School of Medicine
6. Xavier University School of Medicine
7. Medical University of the Americas
8. American International Medical University
9. Spartan Health Sciences University
10. St. James School of Medicine
11. American International School of Medicine
12. American University of Integrative Science
13. Bridgetown International University
14. University of the West Indies

For those people who have relatives in other countries and or citizenship and other countries many times you are able to go to the medical school in that country for little or no cost. For example people with relatives in Italy or citizenships in Italy who are able to go to the Italian medical school may be able to go for free if that is somehow set up by their family. Many times people who's family was born in a certain country or they were born there with his citizenship may be able to go to school for free in most countries.

There are even some countries like Cuba who may not necessarily be friendly with the US who will allow some of the US citizens (specifically

African-Americans) to go to medical school free, because they are aware of the oppression suffered by African-Americans in the United States.

Some of these scholarships are:

1. The National Health Service Corps scholarship and or, Loan repayment program. You can win the national health service Corps scholarship, pay back your time by serving your 4 years for the scholarship, and then after you have finished serving your time to pay a scholarship that you can also do loan repayment and continue to work with the clinics that helps the underserved. These scholarships include the Indian health service Corps scholarship, the national health service Corps scholarship, and the Hispanic health service Corps scholarship if you qualify to receive them.

    The National Health Service Corps Scholarship program is interested in physicians that actually plan to pay the time back. It is not difficult to obtain a scholarship. In my medical school class we had 17 people out of 150 who had this full scholarship that paid all of your tuition and fees and gave you $1000 a month approximately while you are going to medical school. Scholarship now still pays your full tuition but gives you $1389 a month. This is the same for the Indian Health Service Corps Scholarship and the Hispanic Health Service Corps Scholarship. The military scholarships are similar but you have to serve at the military to pay your time back. My disclaimers with the military is the possibility of being hurt by serving in combat or being killed but then again is more dangerous to drive your car on the highway. Don't forget about the uniform health services school of medicine where medical school is again free and you get paid $60,000 + a year while you go to medical school.

2. MLK Martin Luther King scholarship, which is at the Rowan College of Osteopathic Medicine

3. The National Health Service Corps Scholarship, Indian Health Service Corps Scholarship, Hispanic Health Service Corps Scholarship. With the Indian Health Service Corps Scholarship you must be willing to work on reservation for 2 to 4 years to pay the time back.
4. Navy health profession scholarship
5. Army health profession scholarship, Airforce health profession scholarship
6. Institutional scholarships at the particular medical school, like NOVA Southeastern College of Osteopathic Medicine Chancellor scholarship for primary care.
7. And the Uniform Services University School of Medicine where you go to medical school for free except for the obligation that you have through the military for the US public health service. All students study tuition free and paid a $64,000 or higher salary to train as future physicians and medical leaders. They feature an extensive-year-old curriculum that focuses on medical science, disease prevention, health promotion, and leadership training that is nearly 700 hours longer than those found in the US medical schools.

There are scholarships that will pay for your entire tuition as long as you are planning to practice primary care specialties such as internal medicine, family medicine, pediatrics and psychiatry and obstetrics and gynecology. At some medical schools they have what are called Chancellor scholarships and state Chancellor scholarships. These scholarships are school scholarships that will pay for your entire tuition but again you have to specialize in one of usually five primary care specialties. There are versions of these scholarships that are for people with Native American ancestry, and Hispanic heritage in addition to the usual National Health Service Corps scholarships.

Some of the medical schools such as University of Virginia have merit-based institutional scholarships that are available for incoming freshmen and are renewable for subsequent years. The Ross School of Medicine which is an offshore medical school has a merit-based scholarship that is available to incoming freshman with a 3.8 on a 4.0 scale and as stated above old MCAT score of 20, and new MCAT score of 505. In subsequent editions of this book I will probably list more of the actual scholarships. It is your responsibility to decide what medical schools you are applying to and scour the year catalog whether paperback or online for the scholarships that they offer on a merit basis. This will ensure that you will at least have the knowledge of what scholarships are available to you with your particular academic situation.

Adding on– the University of Virginia, and the University of Miami have scholarships for nurse anesthetists training. There may be more programs that have scholarships for this but you will have to investigate. Many times students in the nursing program for work their way through the programs and then after they've qualified for this anesthetists which usually takes 2 years of ICU work they tried to work their way through that schooling also like taking shifts that will help them to pay for the school.

UNDERGRADUATE

This book is designed to ensure that the reader understands our main premise is to be **over prepared** for difficult academic programs that you are trying to enter. This means that if you are trying to go to one of the 5 federal military academies, Ivy League colleges, or any college that is considered tier one, and tier two schools.

You will need to take chemistry in 2 parts, calculus in 3 parts, and physics in 2 to 4 parts if you plan to be a science major this includes computers and engineering courses you can take at a college or community college on weekends or at night. You can also take them during the day if your high school allows for has a co-op program where you can take college courses while you're in your last 2 years of high school. If you're worried about the grades from you can always order the courses were take the courses for no grade but ensure that you save your notes and your old tests for the time you read take the course for a grade. All notes and old tests can also be found in similar material such as the REA and Schaum's outlines (in addition to using Khan Academy!!). The MCAT study books and the AP study books are also helpful when trying to heighten your knowledge of these particular subjects. Remember you can retake courses to improve your GPA, and you can audit courses once or twice if you have a great deal of difficulty with the course to solidify your knowledge and then take the course for grade.

Another example is that taking organic chemistry has been difficult as one of the prerequisites for going to medical school. Usually the 1st time you take organic chemistry you don't do well and you end up taking it a second time. So in your 2nd attempt you look like a genius because you've had it before. This is the same premise that many of your contemporaries who go to the expensive prep schools like Sidwell friends and Georgetown prep are able to take advantage of. Many of the high schools now have AP courses which mimic these prep schools that offer advanced level courses before their graduates go to Harvard and Yale.

This brings me back to my Black Star Man/Woman/Person Initiative. Being a black male I know that African-American men are one of the most underrepresented groups in the medical profession, and there seem to be fewer and fewer African-American males applying to programs (they deserve to be in these programs). Along with that the idea is to be so prepared when they reach those programs that there's no need for any special allowances for them to complete the course of instruction with great success. For those of you who are starting the book at this point at the United States Military Academy, West Point, and the other military academies totaling 5 and number the students in the top 5% of the class where academic stars on the collar or uniform because of their high academic rank. Unfortunately, there have not been a lot of African-American males or females who go to the school and wear the stars.

My solution to this/remedy is to have them reach matriculation with such a level of preparation that it is merely a foregone conclusion that they will be in the top percentage of the class academically. Families who go to these schools generation after generation after generation like they are the neighborhood schools prepare their kids time after time after time by taking the classes that I am talking about calculus, chemistry, and physics like they are the basic courses in their curriculum.

Enough rhetoric. The way to do this is to be over prepared academically by either being in a preparatory program for creating your own preparatory program at a community college by taking:

1. PHYSICS 1-4 — including vectors, kinematics, impulse momentum.

    How to start with position equations and get to acceleration equations by using calculus and then go back the other way from acceleration equations to velocity in position equations again. Doing impulse momentum and realizing that in some problems you need to assume that gravity is 9.8 m/s squared for that velocity 0. Learn how to solve each equation for each variable in the equation so you can solve the equation for any value that you will for. This involves multiplying both sides by quantities, dividing seismic quantities, subtracting same quantity from both sides, and adding the same quantities to both sides.

2. CALCULUS 1-3—integration of differentiation

    Not just these 2 operations but the algebra and trigonometry that is needed to arrive your answer. This mathematics needs to be practiced over and over again as much as you can tolerate it.

3. CHEMISTRY 1-2—Stochiometry, and Balancing equations

    Stoichiometry which is the conversion of units like miles per hour to meters per 2nd or kilometers per hour, and learning to balance equations until you can do it backwards and forwards like it's nothing to you. Take a look at, academies examples in addition to the REA and Schaum's outline books.

4. ORDINARY DIFFERENTIAL EQUATIONS

5. ENGINEERING COURSES, COMPUTER COURSES

It's also a good idea to take one or 2 basic English classes that show you how to do a proper essay which you usually know how to do if you've done the essay for the SATs. But just because you've done that test doesn't mean you know how to write a properly formatted essay.

It is also possible to take the courses for no credit if you wish to AUDIT them. AUDIT means taking the course for no credit. Then the next time you take the course for credit you will have seen the course material already, and very possibly get an "A" grade in the class.

Save the old test and memorize them with the correct answers to the point where you can reproducible test without looking at it, questions and answers.

There was even one student who studied the course work in a test preparation program he was taking - Organic chemistry. He learned it so well during the test prep class that when he finally took it for a grade at his University he got an "A" without any problem.

As previously stated in the medical section there is a method of memory that is very helpful. It is making silly pictures up about the information that you're trying to memorize. Because the pictures are silly they hope you could definitely remember certain aspects of the material that you are trying to memorize. This is in the style of the MADE RIDICULOUSLY SIMPLE SERIES. It takes a little practice to get use to, but once you get the hang of it you can easily remember large amounts of information with good accuracy.

Again, these tools are here to help you if you become over prepared for your program of choice. The more you know about the academics in your program the better off you will be when it comes to completing the course work. Over preparation, over preparation, over preparation. If it was the fate of every African American child to be over prepared academically for any academic, or vocational program then their lives would be much better.

Sometimes when students enter schools that are considered challenging schools to attend they find that some students are doing so much better than them and they wonder how are these other people who are there contemporaries can we doing so much better. Then through investigation may find out that most of these people had for example physics and three parts, calculus in three parts, differential equations, calculus based statistics and probability, and some engineering courses such as electrical and mechanical engineering during their pre-college preparation. Many of these types of preparatory programs are at private schools. For example, one person's freshman year roommate went to two years of community college before attending the top tier college. Another example is that one student literally did three years of an electrical engineering curriculum before attending one of the military academies. His stepfather was a graduate of that academy and gave him the advice of being over prepared for the academic rigors awaiting him at the school. There are families of people who have generation after generation of children that go to these academies and each one is given the academic preparation before they enter that will allow them to navigate the curriculum with ease.

So additional courses for preparation would be:

1. COLLEGE ENGLISH 1-2 – standard essay
   ensure that you are able to write an essay that includes an introductory sentence of introductory paragraph a thesis statement with 3 ideas, 3 paragraphs that have those 3 ideas, and a conclusion that restates those 3 ideas.
2. MICRO AND MACRO ECONOMICS
3. HISTORY - your choice if European, or American or both
4. Language of your choice for example SPANISH 1-2

Make sure that when you are taking the English course that you know how to write a basic essay. It is what we referred to as the M1-A1 method of writing an essay.

Topic Sentence:

_____

Introductory paragraph:

_____

Thesis sentence with three ideas: 1_____2_____3_____

Then three supporting paragraphs taken from the three ideas in the thesis statement:

1. _____
2. _____
3. _____

Conclusion: restating the three ideas from the body of the essay.

In keeping in line with over preparation being the key theme of this book some of the most important information in this book has to do with the help of books that are available for these courses like calculus chemistry and physics and differential equations. Some of them are:

One of my classmates literally taught himself Organic Chemistry from the help books without taking the course. This was because he was taking a prep course. While taking the MCAT prep course he told himself the Organic Chemistry along with the classes that were included in the course and when he took the actual course for grade he got an "A". Learn what the problems are asking and how to solve them or memorize how to do at least 7 to 10 problems per section even if some of the problems are the examples in this section.

1. REA publisher series:
    PHYSICS – – vectors, units of measure, kinematics velocity, acceleration, position/range problems impulsive momentum.
    CALCULUS– – derivations integration, algebra and trade needed to get to the answers.

CHEMISTRY– – stoichiometry, balancing equations
DIFFERENTIAL EQUATIONS

2. Schaum's outline series
PHYSICS
CALCULUS
CHEMISTRY
DIFFERENTIAL EQUATIONS

3. Then there are also other series of books named:
FOR DUMMIES
MADE RIDICULOUSLY SIMPLE– – using silly pictures to
memorize large amounts of information
MADE EASY
SUPER MEMORY SUPER STUDENT by: Harry Lorayne– –
method of memorizing using silly pictures this is the book that
teaches the method.

4. Then there is the KHAN ACADEMY where you can find just
about any type of mathematics or science problem demonstrated
with the correct answer and an explanation on how to do them.
(I actually came up with the idea to do the same thing, but these
guys beat me to it, and they did an excellent job).

The above information is considered the most important in this
book, but there are also scholarships and ways to fund your education
that are as important or more important to some readers. These will be
addressed throughout the book as we did when discussing the Uniform
Services University, and the scholarships for medical school. At the end
of this book we will also try to list some of the scholarships and what
therefore as far as profession. In the second edition of this book we will
try to include a more extensive list of scholarships that are important to
the topics were discussing. Beyond that there are separate scholarship

books that are tremendously useful done by several publishers. The Cassidy scholarship book and Princeton scholarship book.

J. Sargeant Reynolds Community College, much like any other community college, such as Howard County community college, Prince Georges Community College, and Delaware County Community College have programs where the students can transfer many if not all their credits to a four-year university without losing any credits or time in their education. The only problem with that since I wrote this book in 1997 is that many of these community colleges are beginning to realize that people are using them to do their first two years in college, and they are starting to raise their prices in accordance with this knowledge. Since the last sentence was written there have been candidates for president who are suggesting that community college should be free like public school. Hopefully this idea will take hold in the legislation will be passed to allow people to go to community college for free. Some schools have cooperative programs where you can transfer all of your community college credits to your for your school and not to have to retake anything from the 1st 2 years.

Like the Virginia agreement plan between community colleges in Virginia for your schools, phi Theta Kappa - scholarship to pay for the last two years. Community colleges are accredited, and credits can be transferred to a four-year college many times with a scholarship that will pay for your education - - the last two years. Especially from a company that will pay for your school with scholarships or co-ops. In addition now there are many online schools where you could do your core courses and non-engineering courses and transfer to a school for the last two years of engineering courses. University of Phoenix/Strayer University and now a dozen more on line schools that have gained credibility sometimes it seems over some brick and mortar schools because industry has taken to their graduates because of their curriculums and course matter that has been tailored to private industry and government jobs.

Some of the undergraduate scholarships are: UVA has a chancellor scholarship, Virginia State University has a chance the Presidential and Provost Scholarship, and Hampton University has a Chancellor scholarship also. Most of these scholarships are no longer fall scholarships, but some of them are. There are also scholarships from the Naval Surface Warfare Ctr., Mark scholarship MAR C, which pays all of your tuition and gives a generous stipend if you are majoring in science. There are several like this from agencies like NASA Naval surface warfare Center Department of Energy Department of Defense for stem or science, technology, engineering and math. There are also co-ops or cooperative education programs where the agencies will pay for a semester, then you work for semester than they pay for another semester and you work another semester. Some of the agencies or Naval Surface Warfare Ctr., Naval Air Warfare Ctr., Naval Underwater Warfare Ctr., Motorola, Raytheon, Sikorsky, McDonnell Douglas, Lockheed Martin, General Dynamics.

I love these schools because they love me first, and when I needed it the most. When I went to them they welcomed me with open arms. They love and welcome all black students but they love and welcome all students regardless of whether the black white or any other color.

Historically black colleges and universities have played an integral part in the education of minority students throughout the last 150 years. In the 60's to 70's affirmative-action became a thing. This went beyond the original integration of many colleges because of sports like football. And gave African-American students along with all other people of color the opportunity to attend universities that they wouldn't even be considered for because of the color of their skin. This was regardless of their academic achievement and sometimes superior academic accomplishments. But along with this many of the historically black colleges and universities have tried to encourage diversity by having scholarships for Caucasian students. This is a little well-known part of academia. Many Caucasian students who felt like they could not get an education because they were not able to afford it were actually eligible to get a free college education at many of the historically black colleges and universities of which there are over 100. Some of these scholarships or programs still exist and would provide a cost-free education for the Caucasian students who apply to the programs. This could possibly even translate to the HBCUs that have Medical and Law schools.

Places like Virginia State University are great places to study and get engineering, and engineering technology degrees, but they can also help you to prepare to go to a top tier college because their teachers are nurturing and actually concerned about your learning the rigorous material. Then going to an academy and turning yourself into a "star man" even if you aren't Black. It is also a good idea to get your initial engineering degree from a Virginia State University, Hampton University, Howard University, or North Carolina A&T University where the teachers are invested in your learning the course work (and truly care about you), and then go to the Harvard, Yale or MIT for graduate work.

ECPI is one of the schools that has survived unlike DeVry and provides education like engineering that is accepted by the government and private industry. It is currently accredited, but when this book was 1st written it was not along with DeVry. These places are formidable places of education that allow you to acquire a functional working knowledge of engineering and mathematics enabling you to acquire a excellent job with government and private industry companies (In a short amount of time – as little as 2.5 years). Many times this is for people who have had previous experience in the field. The training obtained through the Army Navy and Air Force are gaining more credit with employing companies outside of the services. There are many online schools that will help to provide much of the core curriculum needed to finish and engineering or scientific degree. This is the same with the Army, Air Force, Navy, Coast Guard, Marines. Actually these schools are now credited and able to award recognized certificates and bachelor of science degrees.

Places that have co-op programs and scholarships for undergraduate degrees through doctorate degrees for engineering and stem disciplines if you are working there. Some of the names are: - - United States Naval surface warfare Center(NSWC),(in AWC), (NUWC), Motorola, (NASA), Lockheed Martin, Northrop Grumman, Sikorsky, Hughes Corporation, Ford, General Motors, Boeing, Airbus, Bell helicopter. There are some government agencies that also have scholarships and co-ops (and internships) for students in areas of history, political science, and international relations.

These places have co-op programs that will pay for half of your undergraduate education only with a 3.0 GPA out of 4.0 as far as I know. It used to be only a 2.5 GPA, but I guess they found too many people found out about the program. These programs will also pay for your Masters of science degree and PhD degrees while you work for them. These co-ops can be started directly after high school without winning any scholarships. One of my coworkers was a mechanical engineer went to Clemson University. Not only did he not owe any money after his education was completed, he ended up making $20,000 one year during the work part of his co-op. You will receive full salary while in school, and if eligible will get your full salary and a promotion once you get your degree (Masters or PhD).

ORGANIZATION SCHOLARSHIPS- -

Part of what inspired this book was that every year approximately 15,000 cadets and midshipmen go to school for free. Every year at the 5 federal military academies in return for military and maritime service these people are afforded a free for your education and possibly the chance to go to graduate school before doing the service. Please remember that is always a possibility of being wounded or killed in combat or noncombat action or training that's my disclaimer.

Agency - Naval Surface Warfare Center - co-ops, scholarships, and STEM programs– internships.

I would like to concentrate on the school based scholarships first. These are the scholarships that many people do no know about:

- At Virginia state University there is the Presidential scholarship, and the Provost scholarship. These $10,000 awards are for students who pursue a college preparatory course of study in high school, and maintain a 3.2 grade point average, and 1100 SAT score for the Presidential scholarship, and a $6500 award for a 3.0 grade point average, and 1000 SAT score for the Provost scholarship. These awards are renewable and usually require that you participate in the honors college, and stay on campus with tuition paid. Some of these awards also include a stipend for spending money.

These military schools that are not military academies have scholarships that are not ROTC scholarships and do not require any commitment to the military. So if you would like to go to a military school/college (not including military high schools) and not incur commitment you can still go to one of these prestigious schools for free. Military high schools have nothing to do with this book except for being a category for military Academy nomination. Military high schools are completely different story because many parents send their children there traditionally as a means of disciplining them. Back to military colleges - remember that you will go through their 1st year indoctrination program which is similar to basic training in the military. Not completely accurate examples of this are in the books the lords of discipline, dress gray, and fields of honor. But going to the schools is an individual choice and people need to think and act wisely when making a decision to go to one of these schools. Many times these places are considered a good place to start your career regardless of what you go into because of the discipline that is instilled. They are great places to be from, but difficult places to go to. You only want to go to the schools if YOU WANT TO GO!! Not for anyone else.

- Virginia Military Institute has a state cadetship that bona fide residents of Virginia have the opportunity to obtain if they are picked by their state representatives and approved by the board to attend VMI tuition free but you must pay other costs like uniforms room and board. There is also another scholarship that is given for academic excellence starting from High School and must be renewed every year called the Institute Scholars Program that pays all official cost.

- The Citadel has a full scholarship called - The Citadel Scholars Scholarship Program supported by The Citadel development foundation. There are 12 full scholarships to South Carolina residents and 6 to residents of other states. All expenses that they cover are listed in the catalog. The Citadel also has a program where they encourage military veterans to apply and attend without being part of the regimental system – the corp.

- Norwich University has a President's Scholarship that pays tuition room and board for four years. For all four years to qualify for consideration applications must post a minimum 3.0 GPA in high school to renew the student must maintain a 3.0 cumulative GPA. This scholarship goes to one cadet and one civilian student.

- There are many other institutional scholarships at the over 2500 universities that are available to incoming students and students that are already attending the University. You have to investigate, and search for the institutional scholarships that your school's if they have any.

- University of North Georgia military school – – also has a scholarship that can possibly give you $85,000 over 4 year period if you're a Georgia resident. In addition, there is the leaderships scholarship that gives $3500 a year.

- Virginia Tech – – is also a school that used to be solely a military college but now admits and has for a long-time civilian students. They also have institutional scholarships that are available, but you must investigate. Virginia Tech is a little unclear about their merit-based scholarships when I tried to investigate, but I'm sure you can find out more information.

- Texas A&M University – – is also a school that used to be completely military but now has and has had for a long time civilian students. They also have institutional scholarships that are available but you must investigate. Texas A&M has a presidential scholarship that can give you $3000 per year for 4 years. It has the Lechner scholarship that will give you $2500 per year for 4 years. It has the McFadden scholarship that will give you $2500 per year for 4 years. It has the century scholarship that will give you $5000 per year for 4 years. And the presidential achievement scholarship that will give you $2500 per year for 4 years.

This same type of scholarship exists at University of Virginia, VirginiaTech, and Virginia Commonwealth University. It is called an **institutional scholarships**, or merit based scholarships. Most schools have a version of this scholarship, but I am sad to say, since the original inking of this book. Many of the full scholarships have been made into partial scholarships, decreased in value, or eliminated altogether. The military schools may or may not have the same weight in their names as Harvard, Yale, Cornell, University of Miami, University of Maryland, Virginia Tech, Howard University, Florida A&M, North Carolina A&T. Tactics for preparation to go to the schools are useful at any of these high-level schools. The year that the author went to the West Point prep school the number one cadet candidate that year academically did not graduate from the prep school. He left and went to Harvard. When you academically prepare yourself as outlined in this book you will be prepared to go to any University.

Yet, there are still dozens of schools that do have merit-based scholarships that cover full tuition, room and board, and some of the awards still have a stipend for spending money attached. Researching the web. I was able to find that Baylor University has similar scholarships if you score very high on the SAT or ACT and list them as your first choice. They are awards go as high as $22,000 for the year. If you earn a presidential scholarship everything will be paid for.

A superior GPA at a community college is probably much more influential than equivalent grades from a high school. Unless you are involved in the world of the privileged and are attending Sidwell friends, Georgetown prep and the like high schools. Community college work shows that you are already capable of doing college-level work successfully. In addition there was an article that set up to a third of the students who attend Ivy League schools are legacy or the children of donors making getting into those schools for those kids no different than going to a state school or community college. Many of them have dedicated tutors and once they get in it is a foregone conclusion that they will graduate. How well they graduate as far as GPA will be up to them and their assistants. I don't believe that there is any impropriety like people taking the test for them which Donald Trump was accused of but they do have helped that is not afforded other students.

When you have a **scholarship, co-op, or internship** you come out with an engineering degree and an opportunity for advancement paid for the agency you work for and a guaranteed job if there are spots available. In this section we will talk about becoming an engineer even though I was a physicist just like the guidance counselors who talk about becoming doctors when they have never tried to become a doctor or end up as your pre-health advisor was never having gone to medical school.

ENGINEERING

Electrical engineering,

Introduction:

electrical engineering is the study of electronics and its uses. It generally deals with the study and application of electricity, electronics, and electromagnetism. It also has a wide range of subdivided feeds, including computers, digital computers, telecommunications, robotics control systems and radiofrequency engineering. Electrical engineers are professionals that deal with design and construction of electrical circuits, and study the application electrically, electronics, and electromagnetism. It can be electrical or computer engineering.

How to become one:

there are several ways to become an electrical engineer. This field involves a good deal of mathematics which is not prohibited if you put in the effort to learn it and practice it just as you would any other sport.

1. Go to community college and study their electrical engineering (or electronics technology) transfer curriculum (which include CALCULUS, CHEMISTRY, PHYSICS, and DIFFERENTIAL

EQUATIONS), which usually encompasses the courses is needed in the first two years of electrical engineering, including calculus, chemistry, differential equations, and physics. You can also study electronics technology, which in many community colleges have a similar curriculum to the engineering transfer curriculum. Many times the teachers at these school are committed to teaching you the information the best they can. So that you will make them look good when you transfer. This is usually the opposite at engineering freshman programs at the big schools in these programs where many times they are looking to eliminate a certain number of freshmen from the program (under the guise of them not being able to cut it).

2. There are also schools like ECPI that can help you to achieve your goal of getting a bachelor of science in electrical engineering in as little as 2.5 years. These programs are usually tailored to people who have trained in or worked in the discipline previously such as former military, and people who were previously enrolled in similar programs.

3. Then there is the traditional four-year school that has a electrical engineering major, and hence curriculum. This ranges from MIT, Virginia Tech, Ressler and many of the other engineering schools. (Notre Dame, West Point, Naval Academy (including nuclear engineering), Coast Guard Academy, Merchant Marine Academy, Air Force Academy, Texas A&M, North Carolina A&T).

What they don't tell you:

If you're trying to go to a high-powered school to graduate with an engineering degree many times it is better to do the first two years of the training at a community college or in HBCU where the teachers are nurturing and want you to succeed. Many times at the big programs they are looking to eliminate people in the first two years and pretend that they need to weed people out. To them not everybody can be an engineer, but that's a fallacy. People who truly desire to become engineers and are willing to put in the work are usually going to be more successful than others who have an affinity for it but don't work as hard.

You will read this over and over again in this book that **over preparation** is the key to exceptional performance. Once you enter these programs. The instructors may even ask how do you know some of this, and then it is up to you to determine how much you want to tell them about your background.

This is the key to my Black Star Men/Women (or black cadets/ minority or underserved cadets that are not privie to the information that will allow them to academically before they arrive at the military academy). This information would allow these black star men to become a more common site. To have even the African-American football players at West Point achieve the highest grades possible, it would be best if they were take the calculus, chemistry, and physics, before they entered the Academy. Not just taking it, but actually learning it the best that they can to the point of being able to teach it themselves. This would also be the same idea for African-Americans (not to say that all African Americans are disadvantaged) or any disadvantaged individual would be able to navigate the academic curriculum at any Tier 1 or 2 University.

There was a time when colleges would recruit players that were exceptional football players, but not exceptional students. They play out their eligibility and then flunck them out of the college. This was allegedly a practice at the military academies (and other schools). Not an official policy, but something that the coaches will do and the administration would turn and blind eye as long as the football team was improving. Or this is how it looked to an outsider. The academies not being the only schools that would do this. The remedy of course would be to assign a tutor to the cadet or student who would help them with (not do) their academics (like the tutor Miss Sue in the movie the blind side). This would've helped the students to perform to standard academically and not just play out their eligibility. Allowing them to graduate with their degree and move on to their careers. These tutors could be professional tutors, or tutors from the University that would be assigned to that student to help them do the best to ensure that they'll graduate. It would seem that if they were going to invest all the money that it took to give them a full scholarship so that they could play a particular sport then it would make sense to give them a tutor at a fraction of the costs to help them to graduate.

So, when I say West Point that is the place that you substitute the name of any high-level school that you are trying to go to. Whether it is an Ivy League school like Harvard or a private institution like Notre Dame, or a state University like Ohio State University. Your over preparation will not be a waste of time.

For us, average people/normal people who don't have the advantage of going to a private high school/prep school, the way to balance things out or to be on an even keel is to take college prep, advanced placement (AP)courses in a public high school, or community college courses while we are in high school to ensure that we get the level of education that is needed for these top-tier schools. Or after high school before you transfer to or start over at your new school. You cannot transfer to the military academies usually. Sometimes there are exceptions decided by the people in the Pentagon. And many times people decide not to transfer into their high-level schools and would rather read take the courses that they took previously to ensure a high GPA that is comprised of the courses that they know that they will do well in. The higher the GPA the better.

Engineering, electrical engineering, electronics technology curriculums in community colleges are usually in line with the courses that I am naming above. They have the CALCULUS, CHEMISTRY, and PHYSICS in their curriculum that I'm talking about. Even the basic engineering courses are included and these courses will give an introduction to the engineering courses that are at the top-tier schools. It is important to also recognize that English and writing skills, history, and foreign language are important so that the student will not have difficulty with the various writing assignments.

Simply because you are academically prepared and able to achieve a high or excellent GPA in these schools because of your superior preparation does not mean that you will be treated the way you wish to be. These are competitive environments and your being unexpectedly good at the course work may not be welcomed. There is a stereotype that people of color or from underserved backgrounds are not as good academically, but this is not true. All brain matter is the same color! But be emotionally prepared not to be welcomed with open arms and these competitive environments.

There are some students many times people of color from other countries who believe that if they are academically equivalent or superior to their majority counter parts that they will gain acceptance from their academic excellence, but this is sadly a mistaken assumption. Once they realize that you are academically competent or superior than they will dislike you even more because you are legitimate competition for the degree that you are trying to obtain.

Ways to pay for school:

I understand that some of this is repetitive, but this was all born out of the idea that there are several thousand people that go to the five United States military academies in this country for free every year. So not only do they get a top-notch education and a job guaranteed afterwards, but it doesn't cost them anything and they actually get a salary while going to school. I began to think about what are the other opportunities for scholarships at these types of schools and at nonmilitary colleges in this country. Hence my need to let everyone know about this opportunity especially those students who think they cannot afford a college, graduate, or professional school education.

There are scholarships partial and full:

- School based scholarships – – presidential scholarships
- Major based scholarships – – engineering/science scholarships, Department of Defense, Department of Energy.
- ROTC scholarships - Navy, Airforce, Coast Guard, Army scholarships, Marine PLC, Coast Guard College commissioning program, Maritime programs in the country.
- Organization scholarships – – Divine 9 give scholarships for academic achievement, and scholarship books such as Cassidy have hundreds of these scholarships that are available to a wide variety of people.
- Agency - Naval Surface Warfare Center - co-ops, scholarships, STEM programs, internships.

I would like to concentrate on the school-based scholarships first. These are the scholarships that many people do no know about. At Virginia state University there is the Presidential scholarship, and the Provost scholarship. These awards are for students who pursue a college preparatory course of study in high school, and maintain a 3.2 grade point average, and 1100 SAT score for the Presidential scholarship, and 3.0 grade point average, and 1000 SAT score for the Provost scholarship. These awards are renewable and usually require that you participate in the honors-college, and stay on campus with tuition paid. Some of these awards also include a stipend for spending money.

This same type of scholarship exists at University of Virginia, VirginiaTech, and Virginia Commonwealth University. It is called an institutional scholarship, or merit based scholarships. Most schools have a version of this scholarship, but I am sad to say, since the original inking of this book. Many have the full scholarships have been made into partial scholarships, decreased in value, or eliminated altogether.

Yet, there are still dozens of schools that do have merit-based scholarships that cover full tuition, room and board, and some of the awards still have a stipend for spending money attached. Researching the web. I was able to find that Baylor University has similar scholarships if you score very high on the SAT or ACT and list them as your first choice. They are awards go as high as $22,000 for the year. If you earn a presidential scholarship everything will be paid for.

Engineering - Mechanical / Civil / Aeronautical / Nuclear

What they are:

Mechanical engineering has to do with temperature and pressure with materials and how they are affected by the environment provided. They build and test mechanical and thermal devices. As a physicist I worked with this type of engineering most.

Civil engineering has to do with shaping the out door environment to a useable space like creating road ways and airports and or shaping the land scape to build buildings or structures.

Aeronautical engineering has to do with creating structures / airplanes that can travel through the air more efficiently with greater lift and sustainability of flight.

How to become one:

Again the general way to become and engineer is go to the engineering program at a school that has the curriculum, but there are options. Go to a 4 year engineering program, go to a community college program for two years (taking CALCULUS, CHEMISTRY, PHYSICS, and ORDINARY DIFFERENTIAL EQUATIONS) and then complete the next two years at a four-year institution which is the most cost-efficient way to complete a lot of your schooling.

1. Go to community college and study their Mechanical/Civil / Aeronautical/Nuclear engineering transfer curriculum, which usually encompasses the course is needed in the first two years of Mechanical/Civil /Aeronautical/Nuclear engineering, including calculus chemistry, physics, and ordinary differential equations (till you know them like the back of your hand). You can also study general engineering or their electronics technology, which in many community colleges has a similar curriculum to the engineering transfer curriculum. Many times the teachers at these school are committed to teaching you the information the best they can. So that you will make them look good when you transfer. This is usually the opposite for your big school programs where many times they are looking to eliminate a certain number of freshmen from the program.

2. Then there is the traditional four-year school that has a electrical engineering major, and hence curriculum. This ranges from MIT, Virginia Tech, Ressler and many of the other engineering schools. (Notre Dame, West Point, Naval Academy (including nuclear engineering), Coast Guard Academy, Merchant Marine Academy, Air Force Academy, Texas A&M, North Carolina A&T). and a whole host of other colleges that we may name further on in the book like Howard University.

Kaplan courses are available for test preparation, but require a great deal of individual initiative in order to make the money you spend worth your while. I would recommend that you have a study buddy, or a tutor that goes over the passages and answers with you, at least twice a week for several months, so you can get good use of the materials.

Pick out information if possible. That is relevant to you, doing well and memorize these pieces information as you go along by whatever memorization method you have. There are several ways people memorize information. They repeated until they learned it from memory, they make mnemonics to memorize the information, and they can use the Super Memory Super Student method of making pictures/silly pictures that help them to memorize the information.

This goes for any SAT preparation, MCAT, or LSAT preparation. As you all probably aware of that there are many types of these entrance exams for the various professions out there. From firefighters, postal workers, policeman, military pilots. There are entrance exams and aptitude tests. All of these tests can be prepared for in the same manner described above, but it takes diligence, the ability to stick to your studying schedule. use the Baron study books to prepare for the exams. There are even community college curriculums for criminal justice, fire science, and private pilot courses in schools.

This preparation is easy for those people who are more obsessed with their chosen professional interests (like it is their hobby) because it takes no effort for them to read about and study information that will help them achieve high scores on the test. Some people would even label those folks as naturals, genius, or ringers - someone who's has done this before. You may have to treat this information like it is your hobby in other words read it study and or play games with it on your phone like you would candy crush.

ROTC:

Reserve officers training course or for becoming officers in the different military services. This course can be taken while at nonmilitary colleges. There is army, Air Force, Navy, Coast Guard, and Marines. There is also a version of ROTC for the Merchant Marine at several schools, including Texas A&M. Again the disclaimer that when you join the military your main job is to fight. During war time to scan result in being crippled wounded or killed in combat, and sometimes during peace.

I am mentioning these programs because many of them provide full tuition scholarships that also include stipends that help with living expenses. This also includes medical schools and law schools because army Air Force and Navy will pay for your medical school professional, and law education along with giving you a monthly stipend for living expenses. These services will also give you full tuition scholarships that will pay for your law school education, along with providing a stipend for living expenses. These programs expected in return that you will serve with them as an officer providing medical legal services for a specified amount of time approximately 5 years active service, and an additional three years inactive reserves. There are also Marine Army Air Force and Coast Guard officer training programs called OCS, PLC, OTS which can be done after you finish your degree or in the case of the Coast Guard during your bachelors degree. You will have to look into the details to see which program will help you pay for your education.

With the military avenues you should want to be in the military. The job of the military is to fight, and you may get injured or killed doing your job.

The public health service/national health service Corps also provides this same type of scholarship for medical education paying all of your tuition, and providing you with a stipend or monthly living allowance of approximately $1400 a month. Unfortunately, some shortsighted Congressman felt that it was necessary to possibly tax this living expense money because he thinks that you're going to make a lot of money in the future. Frankly, that is despicable and is detrimental to the education of the future doctors that are in the program. this is not necessarily so if you plan to serve the underserved population for any length of time.

Military Academies:

Beginning with the disclaimer again. With the academies you should want to be in the military. The job of the military is to fight, and you may get injured or killed doing your job. This is also true in other lines of work. The reason why the section is being given is that the military academies can provide a free education. Every year there are at least 15,000 cadets and midshipmen going to school for free. These schools you will definitely need to be over prepared academically before entering them if you hope to have a good time. You will need to take your calculus chemistry and physics in addition to some engineering courses if possible and English history along with a foreign language. Knowing these courses like the back of your hand will make your academic experience significantly more reasonable. The 5 federal military academies are:

1. U.S. Military Academy, West Point, NY
2. U.S. Naval Academy, Annapolis, MD
3. U.S. Airforce Academy, Colorado Springs, CO
4. U.S. Coast Guard Academy, New London, CT
5. U. S. Merchant Marine Academy, Kings Point, NY

Out of these 5 federal military academies all of them need to have an academic acceptance along with a congressional nomination (or one of the 10 types of nominations), except for the Coast Guard Academy which only requires academic acceptance. When you go to these schools you're going to be busier than most normal four-year colleges. While attending the schools you will also be paid a salary of over $1000.00 dollars a month (just like the Uniform Services University school of medicine), but you have to survive the 4th class system in addition to all the other military traditions while you're there. Rather than talking about stories from plebe year now is time to provide information that is important to obtaining admission to the academies like congressional nominations/nominations of all types:

1. Congressional
2. Senatorial
3. Reserve component nomination
4. National Guard component nomination
5. Active Duty
6. Presidential

7. Vice Presidential
8. Honor ROTC high school unit
9. College ROTC unit nomination – – like from those six on the military schools previously mentioned in the book.
10. Sons and Daughters of deceased or 100% disabled veterans
11. Other Countries Defense Attache
12. Medal of Honor Children

One important thing of note is that the age limits for going to the academies are 17 to 23 years old where they used to be only up to 22 years old. The Merchant Marine Academy has the oldest age of admission for the academies (up to 25 years of age), which helps to extend this opportunity of going to a US Military Academies for those who have decided to do it a little bit later in life. This is also true for many of the other maritime service schools which allow you to go to them and varying ages. Some schools such as the California maritime school will allow ages up to 30 with a waiver for commissioning having had prior service. Any other details you will need to contact them or research it. The school offers a real-world civilian life opportunity as a mariner like Captain of a **cargo /oil for cruise ship**. Or you can work for the oil industry like shell or Exxon. There are also smaller programs and training schools that help you to become things like a **tugboat captain**. These programs cannot be over emphasized. They are the lead up to sometimes very lucrative careers with something that you may love doing.

There are nominations through Congressman and Senators. Usually for each nomination the congressman and senator will make 1 principal nomination and 10 alternative nominations. The alternative nominations are just as good as the principal nominations if the person with the principal nomination does not get an appointment. Sometimes the appointments are kind of dependent upon the needs of the academy. I heard one story that the football coach wanted a particular student to come to the academy and play football, and he was able to get a nomination slot from another state (from the unoffical pool of nominations - usually used for athletes) to give to this particular student so he could come and play football. You are more valuable to the school if you play a varsity sport. Of course they will say that all the students are equally important to them, but that is not necessarily true.

Reserve component nominations and National Guard component nominations are available. Some of the nominations are distributed through the preparatory schools of the academies. The same is true for active-duty nominations.

These nominations make it possible for people from the reserve National Guard and active-duty to go directly to the academy they are academically prepared, and also for them to obtain appointments from the Academy prep school if they need a little more preparation. Now many courses are given online, and with the help that you can get from Khan Academy and the help books REA and Schaum's outline series you can take the courses online while in the service or at home and prepare yourself without going to a classroom. You could do it on your own with just the help of Khan Academy. I will also be coming out with some help material either by book or on disk that will emphasize problem-solving help like solving for different variables in an equation and reducing algebraic equations – – which requires practice.

Presidential nominations number approximately 100 and vice presidential nominations number approximately 5. You can read the catalog to determine how to apply for these nominations.

Honor Junior ROTC high school unit nominations - are available at places like Fort Union military Academy and Valley Forge military Academy which are high schools. Valley Forge also has a component that is a collegiate level of academic training, but nominations are not available from that part through high school unit nominations.

College ROTC units can also give nominations for the Academy to cadets that they think are promising and have the potential to successfully navigate the program.

The Medal of Honor nominations are available to recipients of the Medal of Honor and their children.

West Point, the Naval Academy, and the Air Force Academy have their own prep schools where the First 150 people who are not accepted after the class to the Academy has been accepted are allowed to go to their Academy preparatory schools. Each of these preparatory schools also has 150 reservists National Guard and active-duty cadet candidates totaling approximately 300 cadet candidates at each preparatory school every year.

Looking at the curriculum for the Airforce academy from a couple years ago the first year included chemistry one and two, computer science, engineering mechanics, calculus one and two, and general physics. In the second year the curriculum had aeronautical engineering biology with laboratory, microeconomics, probability and statistics, and physics. Even the Airforce academy preparatory school has many of the courses you need to take before you go to the academy. The naval academy preparatory school at Newport Rhode Island also has many of the courses needed to successfully navigate the first year. The west point prep school now at west point is catching up. They have included some of the sciences that you will see in the first year with their prep school curriculum.

Even though the academy's preparatory school is probably the most sure way of getting into that particular academy you have a larger variety of scientific courses at many of the community colleges around the country. You have a larger latitude for going to any school after the community college and the ability to take some of their engineering curriculum as well as their other scientific courses and liberal arts courses. This 1 to 2 years before you go to your choice of four-year college may be the most important preparatory years that you will spend. The purpose of this paragraph is to let you know that you don't have to limit yourself to going to the funds are federal military academies with this type of preparation you can go to just about any ivy league school or big state school that you wish to go to very possibly on a partial or full scholarship with this kind of academic preparation. You can even go on to one of the more normal state or private schools where there is not as much pressure or competition. This would allow you to probably date a little more and enjoy life a lot more. Many of the HBCU's would welcome some with this type of academic preparation and continue to nurture them to make them the best possible engineer or scientists they want to be. It is very possible that you would end up in their honors college was a possible full financial ride.

PREP PROGRAMS

They also have booster like organizations that will pay for eligible candidates to go to several of the Academy preparatory schools that are outside of the actual services like New Mexico Military Institute, and Valley Forge Military Academy. These places have specific academy preparatory programs. They will allow you to experience some military preparation in addition to academic preparation. There are several of these places not just these two. The year of preparation is paid for by the booster club. Courses such as calculus chemistry and physics are given at these places to help bolster the candidates academic prowess. They also help the candidate to improve on their SAT/ACT scores. The cadets and midshipmen who have had preparatory experiences from the Academy prep schools to the booster supported prep schools and regular colleges sometimes number up to a 3rd of classes acceptances. General George S. Patton used the Virginia Military Institute as his preparatory experience before entering West Point. General Hal Moore of the air cavalry fame studied at George Washington University engineering program before entering West Point.

- For those people who are trying to go to one of the military colleges below except for VMI and the Citadel you can still have the military Academy experience even if you are married and have children. Of course, you can't bring them into the baracks with you but you can still have those social connections that won't bar you from attending the military programs. Rules and policies vary so you have to figure out which programs will allow you to be married and have children if that is your situation. Most of the maritime military programs have different restrictions, but may allow you to have outside children and a spouse (not at the federal academies).

- Be aware that out of the United States Merchant Marine Academy, VMI, Citadel, Norwich, Texas A&M, Virginia Tech military programs you can go to any of the services including NOAA. Out of most of the Merchant Marine programs you can go to almost any service. and go to work for civilian organizations. (With the maritime programs it has to be was something in the maritime industry as previously stated – – for USMMA).

- Realize that most of the officer programs such as OCS/OTS/PLC for Army Navy Air Force Marines and Coast Guard are available out of many civilian colleges including Bowie State University for Coast Guard and Hampton University for Coast Guard. Virginia State University has ROTC for the Army, but you can go to any of the OCS programs once you finish, and that is one example of many of the civilian schools where this is possible. Fort union Military Academy which is an honor military high school, and Wentworth Military Academy in Lexington Missouri, Marion Military Institute Marion Alabama, Georgia Military College in Milledgeville, Georgia, Fishburne Military Academy, and Hargrave Military Academy.

There are other military schools but they are not United States Service Academies.

1. Virginia Military Institute

2. The Citadel
3. Norwich University
4. Virginia Polytechnic Institute
5. Texas A&M
6. New Mexico Military Institute – – also has early commissioning program (ECP).
7. Valley Forge Military Academy - (the reason I included to school is because it has a two-year commissioning program for the Army). You must go on to complete the bachelors degree within 36 months of getting a commission, and there is also the EAP educational assistance program.

Are all military schools that have scholarships that are available and may add up to full tuition coverage with stipends. But with these military schools you do not have to go to one of the armed services. 30% or more of the people that attend these schools do not go on to serve in the military directly after graduation. This means you can have the military school experience and still not go into the uniform services. Norwich University and Virginia Tech were only military schools for many years then day at a passive learning component. These schools have ROTC like the other colleges that are not military academies. These schools usually love if you have an ROTC scholarship. There are several other military two-year colleges and four-year colleges that are available in the US for a total of nearly 25 schools. Some of them are:

1. SUNY Maritime College
2. Maine Maritime Academy
3. California Maritime Academy
4. Massachusetts Maritime Academy
5. Texas A&M Maritime Academy
6. University of New Orleans-naval architecture and Marine engineering
7. Golf Coast Maritime Academy

8. Resolve Maritime Academy
9. Palm Beach Maritime Academy
10. Maritime Institute of technology
11. Maritime professional training
12. Bluewater Maritime School
13. MAST Academy Rickenbacker Causeway

This is an additional paragraph for those who are interested in becoming a tugboat captain and would like to go to the training:

NEI Northeast Maritime Institute – U.S. Coast Guard Approved
Maritime Professional Training, Ft. Lauderdale, FL
Maritime Training Center, Tampa, Florida

Apprentice Mate Program

– 6 Pack Captains License
– 100 ton Masters Upgrade
– 200 ton Masters Upgrade
– Apprentice Mate Steersman

Now it may not be necessary to have over preparation for some of the above schools, but it doesn't hurt to have taken those basic courses for this book which are calculus, chemistry, physics, and differential equations (engineering programs). You will definitely need that kind of preparation for the 5 federal military academies because the goal of this book is not to see you just get in but to complete the course of instruction at the school without any difficulty if possible (to excell at academics). At West Point to course of study is 47 months. Being able to get through some of the toughest months in the beginning (plebe year) with academic ease would make your time there tremendously better because you would actually be able to enjoy the rest of the journey (smell the roses along the way). Now you will definitely run into those people who say that this over preparation idea definitely not necessary. They'll say that they went there with a second-grade education and were able to walk around as star men for most of their semesters. Now of course I am joking - (not a second grade education). These people are obviously not mere mortals, but geniuses. There are people who have photographic memories, and who learn difficult concepts very easily without having had prior preparation. They do exist. The rest of them will be imposters and have had the courses previously but pretend that they haven't regardless of the format. For example some people will take physics in 3 or 4 parts in high school, and chemistry in 2 or 3 parts in high school, and calculus in 2 to 4 parts in high school. Where their teachers took an inordinate amount of time and care ensuring that their knowledge of those subjects was thorough and all-encompassing. For us normal folk who are not afforded that luxury, and need time and experience in certain coursework to do well the advice in this book is invaluable.

One of the cadets who was the son of a general went to the military Academy at West Point and quit after his plebe year. He resigned. He went to a college civilian college, and finished a degree in history. He then returned to West Point and became the First Captain which is the highest-ranking military cadet, and graduated from the Academy. Now having a dad who was a general probably helped, but it shows that the idea of getting extra education before going to or completing the academy is not a new idea. Although he probably left to go live the regular college life – party hardy, and then return to the military school.

Remember applying to these schools are just like applying to any other four-year college unless it's a military Academy. You will need to take ACT and or the SAT. It is a good idea to take test preparation courses by Kaplan or Princeton Review which can be very pricey. They can range from $500 to more than $2500. Also places like Huntington learning center and Sullivan will help you prepare for these tests if you buy their programs in-house. A lot of the cost can be eliminated if you self-motivated and buy the prep books and give yourself a dedicated program of studying them on your own(like a self-imposed study program of an hour to 3 hours a day depending on what you think you need). Some of the books are:

1. Kaplan SAT prep plus
2. Kaplan ACT prep plus
3. Official SAT Study Guide 2020 Edition - by the College Board
4. Cracking the SAT Premium Edition - by Princeton Review
5. SAT Prep Black Book - by Mike Barrett
6. Official ACT - by ACT
7. SAT Total Prep: A Comprehensive SAT Prep Guide - Marks Prep
8. PSAT prep 2020

Putting in the correct answers and reading the explanation of why the answer is correct or incorrect.

I used to think that this was a silly way of studying until I went to college and found out that it was how a lot of people successfully studied for these tests using these prep books, and were getting good grades in their classes with the same method of study. Now I recommend this method. Put in the correct answers next to the questions that you're reading, and you can cover them while you're answering the questions on your own if you would like to. But go to the back of the book or the back of the section and get the correct answers, and after doing this use the correct answers, and go to the explanation of the answers. Studying why the other answers are not correct will help you to avoid the same mistakes on the test, and will help to reinforce why the correct answer is correct. When studying for the boards it also helps to reinforce the concept of what the question is trying to cover. For those of you who disagree with this method of study do whatever is best for you. You can put the answers in whatever area on the page you would like to. If you put them in a line down the page then you can easily cover them with a ruler while you're trying to decide what your answer should be. Remember to read the explanation of the answers after you go over the question to get the maximum benefit from your time.

**People often take the SAT/ACT several times to improve this score. Because currently they allow you to take the test as many times as you would like. I took it as many as 6 times. One of the best strategies for taking these tests including the MCAT is to study one section much more than the others so that you can elevate (Jack up) that score as high as possible. Then when you take it again study a different section and practice that different section as much as possible so then you can elevate (Jack up) that part of your score. If you have time take the test again and again study a different section more than the other sections and try to elevate (Jack up) that part of your scores high as possible. Somewhere in this process usually you will achieve the score that you had your eye on, and that will allow you to get into your program or scholarship that you choose. Someone I know did exactly this method on a ACT was able to elevate his score enough to get a full scholarship to college.

*When practicing for the PSAT if that is something you're going to do, or have your child do make sure that you take the test or in the book several times in order to practice taking the test. Only the 1st time counts for the competition for the scholarships that are available NMSQT scholarship.

Now remember this book is for people who would like help with these tests and application processes. If you already know this stuff or have a better way to do this yourself then do so. I've only had two friends who truly had photographic memories and did not need to study the way that I explained above. They only have to read through the information once and a new it. I usually have to use a few methods are starting to remember the material depending on what type of material it is. Use what ever method that is best for you. In addition to all of this you have to put in the appropriate amount of time for yourself.

Someone who needs a long time to study cannot try to cram and go to a test and be as successful as they would like to be. I used a method of studying the answers with the prep books, and I also use the super memory super student method of making silly pictures which helps me to memorize a large amount of information in one small picture. Now you have to study the picture that you make and actually remember it when you get to the test, and remember what the picture represents as far as the actual course material. Even if you were not serious about your original academic endeavor in high school or college or sometimes professional school you can catch up and make yourself an above average to exceptional student by using these methods of study.

There are a multitude of study materials that are online, some are free, some are not. Again KHAN Academy has a lot of study material that can help. You have to use your time wisely when doing this preparation or extra help. It may require that you not go out with your friends or play your video games, but it can be done.

MILITARY SCHOOL'S FIRST YEAR

During the first year you are a freshman which is referred to as a plebe. As a plebe you are required to live under the fourth class system. This is supposed to be a system that levels the playing field for every one who enters the academy/school.

1. Your four responses are yes sir no sir no excuse sir, and sir I do not understand.
2. You must know the front page of the New York Times, and be able to explain any article with, "sir today it was reported in the New York Times that…." You must know at least one sports article conversantly.
3. You must know the menus of the day saying them with format: "sir for breakfast we're having…:"; "sir for lunch/dinner we are having…"
4. You must eat at attention, one fist distance from the front of the table and one fist distance from the back of your chair.
5. You must be able to answer a question within 2 seconds of being asked after taking a bite of food
6. You can only look at the table while you chew - you can only chew with your hands in your lap - forearms parallel to your thighs and announce meals. Hold the meal up to your right

and say, "sir for dinner we are having baked ziti would anyone not care for a serving of Baked Ziti?" In addition you must announce the beverages, desserts, and know the beverage, ice cube, and dessert preferences of all of the upper class at your table. Also you must cut the desserts into equal sized pieces for the upper class sold if only five or seven cadets want desert then you must cut those pieces evenly. If you fail to perform these tasks you will forfeit your dessert.

7. You must also deliver laundry, mail, and call minutes - which is a verbal countdown to formation. Which goes like this - all of the minute callers must make a simultaneous right or left face to the middle of the hallway and say together, "sir there are five and abut minutes until assembly for dinner formation, uniform is Dress Gray, first class will wear Sabres, the menu for dinner is baked ziti, green beans, macaroni and cheese, a Martha Washington sheet cake -> (at the third minute on the sixth floor) - "this is the last minute to be called for this formation do not forget your lights! 3 minutes Sir!

8. These are just some of the things that are required of a plebe. Also must know the days.

9. In addition, to the 20 credit hours of academics that you take while you go to classes six days a week, and play a sport that is either varsity or corp squad, club squad or intramural. This 20 credit hours is why having had the courses previously would make your life easier unless you know someone who was a cadet you would not know about the fourth class system in addition to the school work.

It is much better to go to these schools worrying about how high an A or a B your going to get out of your classes because you were academically overprepared rather than worrying about passing the courses no matter what the color of your skin. There are actually some old corps instructors who feel that they are part of the hazing chain of command and will torture you with your work if you are failing like they are part of the plebe cadre. Some instructors even talk to one another about who is failing to see if they are failing the same person. You can take these prep courses at a community college, four year college after high school or (nights, weekends, or summers) from your sophomore year in high school through your senior year.

Paying for these schools: well the academies are free for the most part along with a monthly stipend or paycheck, but there are also full scholarships which include tuition and room and board at a lot of the other schools. VMI has a state cadetship that pays for most of that education, the citadel has a similar scholarship, and Norwich has a presidential scholarship. There are also pell grants, student loans that are subsidized and unsubsidized, and institutional scholarships at many of the private and state schools. One such a scholarship is the presidential scholarship at Virginia State university where most of your tuition room and board will be covered by the complete financial package once everything is said and done. This will most likely include you're being in the honors college and honors dormitories. But it is important that you search for these scholarships at your desired institution and it's a good idea to look in Cassidy and Barrons scholarship books. Now there are more than just these two scholarship books but the idea is to put forth the effort to apply for the scholarships you may have to win several of them to cover your expenses.

Some of the scholarships are available are (The Divine Nine):

1. Omega Psi Phi academic scholarships at each chapter
2. Delta Sigma Theta academic scholarships at each chapter
3. Alpha Kappa Alpha academic scholarships at each chapter(High Wanda Sikes!)
4. Alpha Phi Alpha academic scholarships at each chapter

5. Zeta Phi Beta academic scholarships at each chapter (Hi! Sherl Underwood!)
6. Phi Beta Sigma academic scholarships at each chapter
7. Sigma Gamma Rho academic scholarships at each chapter
8. Iota Phi Theta academic scholarships at each chapter
9. Kappa Alpha Psi academic scholarships at each chapter

One example was a man was trying to go to a culinary school he looked through the Cassidy book and was able to apply to nearly 30 scholarships. He won several of them and was able to cover his tuition room and board, and have money to spend on books and other items. This is one this book is important to me because I can hopefully tell other students who were like me and need help won't have to find out after the fact that money was available for them to complete their programs.

This book is slanted towards science majors because that's what I was, but there are scholarships available for people in business especially was business computer mix, and purely business studies. There are internships and co-ops that helped pay for school. What drives the world's business and trade.

When working at the naval surface warfare center I was able to find out that they have a number of scholarships that will pay for education in science. They have stem program scholarships, co-ops, internships that will pay for your undergraduate schooling. If you are able to get a job with them they have programs that will pay for your masters and PhD in addition to paying you your regular job salary while you are studying to get these degrees.

Another important point is that when I worked at the naval surface warfare center as I talked to many of my coworkers I discovered that many of them had gone to community colleges for the first two years of their education. The community colleges were inexpensive and if you were able to obtain a scholarship from Phi theta kappa it would pay for the last two years at a four-year institution. Many of them completed their degrees up at Virginia Tech. Often, they finished their degrees in electrical engineering, mechanical engineering, an aerospace engineering. And when you ask them where they went to school they would say they went to Virginia Tech. And if you did not ask them you would never know that they did their first two years at a community college. Many states have programs where the four-year institution will accept 100% of the credits you acquired at the community college that they have an agreement with. Therefore you can go to J. Sargeant Reynolds for the first two years of electrical Engineering Technology and get to transfer all of the credits to Virginia commonwealth university, University of Virginia, Virginia Tech university, Virginia military institute. As previously stated if you get Phi Theta Kappa or one that is similar to it, it may pay for your last two years of school. Florida and Georgia have **bright future scholarships** where as long as you have a good GPA out of high school and go to a state school you have almost a full ride.

If you did not do well initially in college it is still worth applying to some of the scholarship programs because not every one puts an application and sometimes they have more awards that need to be distributed them people applying. That used to be the case anyway. Now it is possible that they have many more applicants. The agencies are:

1. Naval surface warfare center
2. Naval air warfare center
3. Naval underwater warfare center
4. Army research laboratory / JPL

And there's several others that are government agencies with these awards that will help you to go to school for three or at a greatly reduced price. There are also private industry corporations that will help you with similar awards to finance your education. Some of them are:

1. Boeing
2. General Dynamics
3. McDonnell Douglas
4. Martin Marietta
5. Sikorsky
6. Motorola
7. Raytheon

And there are some other department of defense, and department of energy scholarships that are available.

Places that have co-op programs and scholarships for undergraduate degrees through doctorate degrees for engineering and stem disciplines if you are working there. Some of the names are: - - United States Naval surface warfare Center(NSWC),(in AWC), (NUWC), Motorola, (NASA), Lockheed Martin, Northrop Grumman, Sikorsky, Hughes Corporation, Ford, General Motors, Boeing, Airbus, Bell helicopter. There are some government agencies that also have scholarships and co-ops for students in areas of history, political science, and international relations.

How to obtain a co-op position:

1. Call the personnel office of the agency you wish to apply to (which may no longer be required because most applications are done online)
2. Obtain an application SF171 or the equivalent which is now available online
3. Fill it out, but for the sections that say job experience you put in "see resume"
4. Buy a resume book (or look on line) about how to make a resume from Barnes & Noble's or Amazon and make a sharp looking resume highlighting your strong points

5. If you are applying to a federal agency include an addendum calls detailed description. In this detailed description you list each job just as you did on your resume but you provide a larger amount of detail including if needed what you did on a daily basis at the job, and highlighting all of the things that you think are important this is where you write as much detail about each job as you believe is beneficial to you.

6. On your resume should include your GPA if you think it's going to be helpful to you, if you think that is more beneficial to put the course is a study then put that. An example will be provided below this:

Example–Research scientists: At this facility I hope to monitor research with particular instruments such as the oscilloscope and other electronic equipment which help me to determine the wavelength of certain energy coming from the main experiment. In addition to I recorded this information on software that helped us to analyze the data and create graphs that were indicative of our findings.

Co-ops are essentially overcoming the system where you must know someone to get a job. No industries like entertainment or certain areas of business this book will not help you accept some of the resume or detailed description of us one thing you learn about science is "science is science". You may go to the big engineering schools which have more facilities in and research programs but to learn the basics and physics engineering chemistry as long as you have a good professor they can be learned almost anywhere Virginia state University or Norfolk State University, and North Carolina A&T teach the same physics and has MIT or any other large technical school. The differences at the large schools you will be taught by the graduate assistant with very little actual teacher contact. At places like VSU, and NSU you can and do receive instruction and help from the main instructors which includes department heads. Many people learn more actual physics at the small universities than they do at large universities which have a reputation for science because of their research program not because of the instruction. The 1ˢᵗ black permanent professor at West Point that his degree from Virginia state University - Dr. James Stith. And a lot of first are born out of these institutions of higher learning. Before the 1990s first highest-ranking African-American West Point cadets including the first black first captain's father graduated from Virginia State University - Major General Brooks - retired.

The reason why more actual learning goes on at these smaller institutions of higher learning is that the military academies is that so much is required of the cadet. It is more difficult to actually learn everything they are throwing at you if you are seeing it for the first time so the secret is to have seen it before you get there. The first African American graduate of the United States Merchant Marine Academy was a Hampton University (Institute) graduate first.

STUDY OLD TEST

It's a good idea to have studied all tests to the point where you can do them backwards and forwards inside out so for example in physics you know how to manipulate the equation to get whatever value was being asked. For example in our physics tutorial which is to follow this book we will go over how to manipulate equations to solve for the variable that you want. This is just as you would in algebra class but for some reason it seems more difficult when you're trying to do it for physics problem. Maybe it's just ahead game.

Very Important source of scholarships/funding for your undergraduate degree through your doctorate.

Government agencies such as the Naval Surface Warfare Center have co-op programs that will pay for half of your undergraduate education only with a 3.0 GPA out of 4.0 as far as I know. It used to be only a 2.5 GPA, but I guess they found too many people found out about the program. These programs will also pay for your Masters of science degree and PhD degrees while you work for them. These co-ops can be started directly after high school without winning any scholarships. One of my coworkers was a mechanical engineer went to Clemson University. Not only did he not owe any money after his education was completed, he ended up making $20,000 one year during the work part of his co-op.

This way you come out with an engineering degree and an opportunity for advancement paid for by the agency you work for and a guaranteed job if there are spots available

This preparation is easy for those people who are more <u>obsessed</u> with their chosen professional interests (like it is their hobby) because it takes no effort for them to read about and study information that will help them achieve high scores on the test. Some people would even label those folks as naturals, genius, or ringers - someone who's has done this before. You may have to treat this information like it is your hobby in other words read it study and or play games with it on your phone like you would candy crush.

Military pilots/Civilian pilots:

Much of this information was acquired because people that I know or trying to become military pilots, and some of them did. One of the ways to become an officer which allows you to become a military pilot is to join the ROTC or the officers training programs that are available for the Air Force, Navy, Marines, Coast Guard. The best way to become a pilot for the United States Army and ensure that you're going to fly is to go to the warrant Ofc. flight school. In the United States Army if you become an officer and go to flight school you eventually become the manager of the flight unit which then limits your time in the air as things currently stand. If you go to the warrant Ofc. flight program you gain seniority, but you continue to fly because that is your designated job.

In the Air Force and Navy Marines and Coast Guard the officers usually fly most of their entire careers as long as they stay flight qualified physically. It is probably easiest to be selected (if you are qualified) for pilot or navigator out of Air Force ROTC because that is their main goal to produce officers for flying (fixed wing and rotary winged aircraft) and for the other jobs in the Air Force. Navy ROTC also makes pilots and naval flight officers for the Navy. They also make Marine pilots for fixed wing and rotary wing aircraft.

Aside from the military academies Emery Riddle University seems to be one of the largest producers of military pilots. Although I'm not aware of how many pilots they produce.

In a tribute to the Tuskegee airmen one of the main things to keep in mind when trying to become a military pilot is that many times you need to be over prepared before you apply to these programs. Especially the warrant Officer flight program. It will probably be a good idea to get your private pilot's license for fixed wing and rotary wing aircraft. You should at least do the ground schools for fixed wing and rotary wing aircraft. In addition there are also help books to study for the military flight test by Barron's:

1. Barron's Military Flight Aptitude Test
2. AFOQT Study Guide - Prep and Study Book for the Air Force Officer
3. AFOQT Study Guide 2019 &2020 SECRETS - Mometrix
4. King Flight School, or Sierra Academy - other flight schools in addition to your local flight school.

Disclaimer - Flying aircraft has it's inherit dangers like crashing causing injury or death. You have to make your own decision as to whether you will risk doing the flight portion of flight school. It is up to you.

For the Army you have to past the AFAST test to go to Warrant Officer Flight school. The test book preparation and the ground school for helicopters will most likely be excellent preparation for taking the FAST test. To go to a civilian helicopter flight ground school it cost about $265.00 per hour for a piston powered rotary wing aircraft, and quite a bit more for a turbine powered rotary wing aircraft. For many students were trying to fly any flight time is better than no flight time.

One option is getting a ground course and teaching yourself or taking the ground course at a community college. This is usually for fixed wing aircraft. There are a variety of ways to get ground school courses from walking into your local airport to ordering them from the aviation magazines. It is up to you to determine what quality of instruction you would like. Another option is to read a book on how to fly, study the test prep book for the FAA flight test and look at 1 or 2 videos, in addition to using a stick and rudder simulator, or computer/ video game simulator.

To be overprepared you essentially need to KNOW HOW TO FLY A PLANE, and study the Barron's Military Aviation testing book (or a similar book)before you take the Air Force OTS or Navy OCS programs (in keeping with the theme of this book in being over prepared). Out of the Air Force Academy, Air Force ROTC, and OTS programs that service gets its pilot qualification and navigator qualification candidates. Regardless of what program you are going to getting ground school and flight school experience with you head and shoulders above your competition. Much of the same is true for the Naval Academy, Navy ROTC, and Navy OCS where they get their pilot qualification and Rio qualification candidates. Coast Guard Academy, and Coast Guard officer candidate school along with their college program helped to produce Coast Guard pilots and navigators. Merchant Marine Academy and some of the merchant Marine officer programs in the United States allow their candidates to go to flight school through the Navy and the Coast Guard usually. But because you can join any service from the merchant Marine Academy you can also become an Army or Air Force pilot. The Marines go to flight school with the Navy. Coast Guard college student pre-commissioning initiatives scholarship is also available at civilian colleges (CSPI).

The ways of becoming a civilian pilot are numerous. You can go to a flight school that has private pilot programs and flight instructor programs like American Aviation in Manassas Virginia. You can go to helicopter flight school like American Helicopters in Manassas Virginia. As a fixed wing pilot can go on to get your qualifications to fly commercial airlines or cargo planes like for UPS and FedEx, and the helicopter schools will allow you to fly for commercial helicopter entities. Going to these schools can cost as much as going to a regular university, but there are usually scholarships and student loans that are available. There are projected to be shortages of pilots for fixed wing and rotary wing aircraft in the future because it's not an easy thing to do or to qualify to do.

OCS:

This information is people who are interested in joining the military as an officer after college, or from being an enlisted person. You can also do this through ROTC and academies. I believe that this is already been discussed in the book but there is officer candidate school or OCS (OTS for the Airforce). Disclaimer: You should want to be in the military if you do any of these programs. The job of the military is to fight, and you may get injured, crippled or killed doing your job. So it is not just a way to get a free education, and you should be aware of this. OCS is a vehicle to become and officer for enlisted men without interrupting their career.

It is a school that is approximately 8 to 14 weeks long depending on what school you going to and it is a school where they will change you from a civilian to a military officer by teaching you all the traditions and the military skills you need to be a basic officer. In the Navy and Air Force many times the OCS may be geared towards her becoming a pilot, but in the Army is usually geared towards her becoming a line officer that works with the infantry or in support of the infantry.

There are several ways to apply the OCS. If you are in enlisted man you have to apply to your commander, and if you're civilian your recruiter will usually help you through the application process. Many times the OCS officer is more respected than the ROTC officer or the military academy officer because many times the OCS officer was a enlisted men for a few years before applying to OCS. Many times enlisted men like OCS officers because they know what it was like to be in enlisted man before they became an officer that gives orders to enlisted man. They truly know the woes and how the enlistment feel on a day-to-day basis because they were invested for years.

Playing sports and doing extracurricular activities:

Everybody knows about how football basketball or baseball player who goes to any college and is able to get a full scholarship. Even at the US military academies there star athletes are given preferential treatment when it comes to the plebe year, eating at Corps squad tables, and being treated better by the upperclassman than most of the regular cadets. At the military academies all cadets must play a sport, but many of them were also varsity athletes in high school before they arrived at the military academies.

This gives you the ability many times to have a easier time at your school, and easier time getting tutoring, and better treatment by the administration. They are less likely to kick you out of the school for any reason because of your athletic prowess. Remember that how good you are at some of the sports can make or break whether you will stay at the school, go there with a full scholarship, and have a professional athletic career after graduation. At one time the academies refuse a pool of nominations to admit star athletes that would help to bolster their athletic (football) program. Not sure if they still have this pool of unused nominations from states that have an overage/surplus of nominations.

Getting accepted with constant phone contact:

Many people will apply to the school or even a job and never call the recruiting office. I found that with most schools if you call to get updates on the status of your application it shows that you are interested and is a positive thing. But you have to be careful because some schools or admission offices look at your calling as a nuisance and try to turn it into a negative thing.

Whatever school you going to I would test the waters by calling the admissions office and seeing if you can talk to your side admissions officer. If you are able to talk to you admissions officer, and many times it is the same admissions officer it is probably a good thing if you call for regular updates on your file for admission. If you call and you get an annoyed secretary who is constantly trying to connect you with your admissions officer or admissions crew then I would not call as often because it may be considered a negative thing to give the admissions secretary and other staff too much to do.

Financial aid and federal application:

The first thing that you have to do is fill out your FAFSA form for financial aid. This allows you to become eligible for loans grants and school scholarships commonly known as institutional scholarships.

This reminds me that the NMSQT is one of the earliest opportunities to get a $2500.00 scholarship to college. It is the PSAT that allows you to enter the and NMSQT competition. Since the days that I took the PSAT there have been several additions to the test. There is the PSAT 8&9, and there is the PSAT10. These are easier versions of the actual PSAT that you take in grades 8, grades 9, and grade 10 in preparation for the actual PSAT. They are supposed to give you an opportunity to prepare for the actual PSAT that counts for the NMSQT.

The federal financial aid form is also a gateway to the school-based scholarships/institution scholarships at the particular school that you are applying to if any exist.

Old Test:

One of the main things you can do depending on how your school is set up is get the old tests to study especially in science and mathematics courses. If you can start looking at these even before you get to the school it will be of great benefit. Many colleges have a big brother or big sister system or a mentor system where the students that were in the classes before you save the old tests and it's okay to study them.

The military academies usually have the old test in the study/poop room will where you can either have a copy of the old tests to work on. Especially in courses like physics with mathematics if you go over these questions and learn them like the back of your hand many times the test question that you have in the class will be very similar maybe asking for a different variable. In mathematics and physics and chemistry engineering many times the algebraic manipulation of the formula is going to be the key to finding the answer to the problem. In more advance areas of physics many times learning how to do a derivation from a previous tests for a problem from a previous tests will be of great benefit when taking the test that you have to take in your class.

In professional school especially medical schools usually there is a binder or a bank of old tests that you can obtain, that everybody is privy to and it is a big help when getting ready to take your tests. Even though this is a tremendous advantage that is usually allowed at many programs it is still better to come in there – to your program or curriculum having had many of the same courses as previously stated in the book if you study pharmacy or biomedical sciences or physiology or pathology before you get to medical school medical school will be much easier usually.

Flight schools and programs:

As previously stated in the military flight school section is wise to learn how to fly a plane before you try out for the military flight programs. You can take your flight courses at the local airport or take the ground instruction through the courses that are available and pilot magazine like the King flight course, and/or the Sierra academies. Any of these programs that teach you ground school are good. Then getting your flight hours will be up to you as far as getting your private pilot's license and helping you to truly understand how to fly a plane. Simulators are also good.

And the disclaimer sentence in this particular paragraph is to remember that planes don't always work the way they're supposed to sometimes they malfunction and a crash can either hurt too badly cripple you or kill you so be aware of that before you start getting a plane to go fly so you can pass the military flight test examination.

Now for those of you want to be civilian pilots pretty much same rules apply you can go get your private pilots license which will be very helpful before you get into whatever other program you need to get into the fly. They do have flight academies and one of the big schools to go to now for flight is Emery riddle. They have a excellent flight program and they produce a lot of civilian and military pilots. Now it's up to you to research where there are other good flight schools, and you should pick the one that's best for you as far as price and what's being offered as instruction.

Architecture:

There are several historically black colleges and universities that offer architecture as a major one of them is Hampton University. There are quite a few schools that offer architecture as a major but it will be up to you to research your program before you go to see if it will be a good program that you believe you can graduate from. It does you no good to get into a "good program" and you don't graduate from. That's true for engineering programs, and any medical program that you may be trying to get into. It does you no good to go to Harvard medical school and flunk out. So if you plan for a high-level school really any medical school is a high-level school you need to be overprepared.

Study techniques:

Using notecards is a good way to take your work wherever you go so you can study whenever you get the chance. Writing a prompting word on the front and more details on the back that are needed to be known as a way to make up your notecards so you can study when ever you get the chance including taking a break in the student union or hanging out at the coffee shop. You can keep the notecards in your back pocket without having to carry around your computer or any bulky books.

When I was in school there was a videotape of a course called where there's a will there's an "A" day and that Prof. discussed the politics of college. He said that it is good to investigate a course before you take it to ensure that you get the best teacher for the course - the teacher that the students before you put at the course recommend. It is good to try and let the teacher know that you have been studying the work and that you have a few questions even if they are really questions that you need to ask. You let the instructor know that you are interested in doing well in the course and that you're putting in the effort. In addition it's a good idea to ensure that you do all of your assignments early soon as you get them - do not procrastinate at all. Following these rules and a few other simple rules will almost ensure that you do well in the course if you have a reasonable instructor. If you have an unreasonable instructor you will most likely have difficulty getting a good grade in the course no matter what you do unless you are one of those folks with a photographic memory.

Speaking of a photographic memory: one of the best books that I read took me about 2 days to read and cost me less than $10. It actually costs around $2 if you get it used off of Amazon or at the time I got it all for the Barnes & Noble's website. It is super memory super student by Harry Lorraine. The made ridiculously simple series of books is based off this method of memorizing. In this book he teaches you several techniques to memorize, but the most useful memory technique for me was making silly pictures that I made up to memorize large amounts of information. This technique is extremely useful if you have an oral examination or an exam where you are required to regurgitate a lot of detailed information. If you get really good at it you can nearly appear to have a photographic memory as he used to demonstrate in his old infomercials. He has methods of remembering numbers by using letters would seem to be somewhat useful but for me the silly pictures with the best.

One of the ways to avoid necessarily having to learn large amounts of new information once you get to your professional school is to have taken much of the course work before you get to your professional school as previously stated in other examples like pharmacy school, biomedical science Masters, Masters degrees or even PhD's in physiology pathology pharmacology. If you follow this advice and do well in these endeavors I don't think that there is a medical school that you will have difficulty getting into and through.

Education's dirty little secret:

This secret may not seem like a secret but education is not equal. Education you get in the southeast of DC at Ballou high is not the same (even though it should be – it is supposed to be) as the education you're going to get at Georgetown prep up in Bethesda at $40+ thousand dollars a year.

This is a repeat of what I was saying before the learning chemistry in 3 parts, physics in 3-4 parts, calculus in 3 parts are offered at these high-level schools where the teachers truly take time to teach you these courses so you know them by the back of your hand if you want to put in the effort. Many of the inner-city schools that are underserved it's difficult to even get the students to be quiet in the classroom so you can learn. Piping up to say that they are misbehaving or keeping you from learning is nearly signing a warrant for them to set upon you or a variety of other unpleasant things.

Law school preparation and scholarships:

Over preparation for law school was for a long time a problem that I was trying to figure out. While I am not a lawyer I have cousins and friends who are lawyers, and judges, but one thing I noticed is that they never talk about what you learned in law school. This section is dedicated to my daughter who is trying to go to law school. This prompted me to look at the curriculum of law schools that are on their university websites. Looking at a few law schools such as North Carolina Central University, Columbia University, Nova Southeastern University Shepherd and Broad, Howard University, and a few others I realize that many of the courses were the same as the courses in the curriculum to become a paralegal from a community college program. There are also graduate courses of instruction with similar curriculums like the one at George Washington University.

There is also a preparatory program called the **Charles Hamilton Huston** program that is available at Georgetown University. This program is available during the summer.

If you are in a pre-law curriculum in a college I would venture to guess that it is just as good as going to one of the programs that I am proposing, but that is up to the individual.

I would endorse taking one of these paralegal programs especially the ones that are filled with a lot of courses that are similar if not exactly the same as the ones in the law school curriculum. Having reviewed several law school curriculums, and paralegal curriculums at some community college you will want to pick a program that includes the following courses that seem to be in the law school programs:

Civil Procedure
Tort Law

Civil Litigation/Procedure
Contracts
Legal Writing / legal briefs writing
Criminal Evidence
Property / Estates and Trusts
If possible take a course in <u>Constitutional Law</u>

Additional courses to take if available:

These courses I found in the Anne Arundel Community College paralegal and legal studies program, and there are probably several paralegal programs that have similar courses and have a good number of these courses that you can take to over prepared yourself for school - if that's possible. The idea is to get into one of these law schools preferably the one that you want to get into and know enough about the courses that it's not a question of passing but a question of how high an "A" your going to get or if your going to get a "B"

Litigation
Legal research, writing I &II
Legal ethics
Business law
international law and human rights
administrative law
employment law
mediation and alternative dispute resolution
real estate law
intellectual property
bankruptcy law
civil rights law
healthcare law
Estates and trust
appellate procedure
domestic relations

The courses or similar courses are what seem to be in the first - going on to the second year of law school. Unfortunately, some of the pre-law program curriculums do not have the courses that the paralegal programs have. I am not sure why they don't have similar courses to the same courses that you will need in law school, but there are a lot of things in academia that don't make sense. As stated it is probably a good idea to take a course in Constitutional Law. The goal is not just to get into Law school, but to also do well in at least the first year.

The prices of these programs will obviously vary. The graduate program that has many of the same courses will cost $20,000.00 where the community college courses may cause you a total of $2500.00.

1. I would even advise that if you are trying to become a lawyer that one of the quickest ways to do so would be to go a community college and take that curriculum for paralegal, which should be very inexpensive because it is at a community college, and very directed because of the courses that are named above. You must ensure that your paralegal curriculum that you join does have the key courses that are discussed above or have the courses that match or are very similar to the law school program that you're trying to get admitted to. Try to get a job or part-time job or volunteer if you have to the time as a paralegal if you think it will help you.

2. Then you could essentially finish any kind four-year completion of your bachelors degree. It depends how specific you want to be in the last 2 years. You could join a prelaw program, a curriculum of criminal justice for your bachelors degree, or find a University that has a lot of similar courses to the law school you trying to go to and get a general degree if it is available packed with all the courses that you think may help you in law school. One particular paralegal program at Anne Arundel community college has a plethora of courses that will

be useful once you enter law school. There are possibly many other programs with relevant helpful courses to help you get through law school with the highest grades possible, but it is up to you to investigate.

As stated previously in this book if you have a better way to do it then you don't need to be reading the book. Lots of folks are people of means where they have parents or family members who will pay for all of this schooling and cost is literally no object. This includes getting tutors, clerkships, and any kind of preparation that they may desire without worrying about how to pay for it. There are actually some people who grow up around law offices because their parent or parents are lawyers, and if they work in the law office next to paralegals and other law professionals then they may already be prepared for law school without having a lot of formal training.

Again the least expensive way, and possibly the most efficacious is going to a community college that is inexpensive and taking the two-year paralegal program with as many electives as you can fit in, and then finishing your four year degree with a prelaw program or a major that you believe has the courses that will help you get through law school as easily as possible. for many law schools you can even do a generalized degree with no particular major as long as you take the courses you think you're going to need to get in and through successfully. Some schools you have to adhere to the advice of your prelaw advisor.

You can major in just about anything you want to, history, international relations, English, sociology for example, and then take law school or medical school preparatory programs to properly prepare yourself for the rigors of a professional Law program. Remember there are those people who have photographic memories, or abilities to study something and committed to memory with ease. If you are unfortunate enough to encounter one of these people and listen to their advice on what to do before you go to law school - most likely telling you to hardly prepare or have a light preparation course, then I feel for you. It is up to you to do your research understand your abilities, and realize the intensity of these programs, and per your abilities prepare yourself as much as you can.

If you enter "law school full tuition scholarship" into a search engine some of these search engines will come up with as many as 10 pages of full tuition scholarships for law school - some of the entries will be repeats. Then you can decide what law school you prefer to attend, and what law school you believe you have the scores to get into, and go to that University that you think will give you the greatest opportunity for success.

> Community college
> paralegal program
> complete your four degree
> study criminal justice
> study prelaw program
> study electives that will help you successfully complete law school
> search for scholarship money (like Phi Theta Kappa scholarship)
> Aim for a full tuition scholarship to law school
> Military scholarship (disclaimer - military's job is to fight you can get hurt or killed in combat if you are sent to fight)
> law school scholarship
> third-party sponsor scholarship

HBCU

I love these schools, and they showed me love first when they didn't have to. They build me up when I needed it the most. This is possibly the most important section in this book. It certainly was for me. These schools were founded at a time when African-Americans were not permitted to go to the Majority of colleges that existed. That was also a time when Howard University, and Grambling were football national champions. Make no mistake, you can go from your first day of college or pre-college to the completion of any doctorate degree at these amazing institutions! Since this humble beginning they have created some of the greatest professionals in this country. People have heard that only black people can go to these schools, and nothing is farther from the truth. These schools from the beginning have been all inclusive of anyone trying to go to college. Some of these schools in line with the affirmative action policies offer diversity scholarships to white students.

When I went to college there was a white student (one of many) who went to college with a major in Biology, and was not only able to get his B.S. in Biology, but earn a full scholarship to the Medical College of Virginia.

These schools have teachers that are very nurturing. When you walk in there and say that you want to be a doctor, a lawyer, or an engineer they did not say well you have to make it through me first, or you'll never make it. These teachers say let's see what we can do to get you to that goal.

When this cadet that I know left West Point a Captain Diggs bumped into him on north area. He told that cadet make sure you don't stop your education when you leave here. You are one of the top academic competitors in the nation. The cadet asked where did you go to school, and Captain Diggs said he went to Norfolk State University. As soon as the cadet left the Academy he planned to enroll at Norfolk State University. Norfolk State shared a ROTC program with Virginia State University where the program called its home. So, the cadet who wanted an ROTC scholarship enrolled at Virginia State University.

At many of these schools there are institutional scholarships. At Va. State Univ. they have the Presidential scholarship that will give up to $10,000 dollars for a GPA of 3.2 on a 4.0 scale along with a SAT score of 1100 for the old test and the new test score of 1170, or ACT composite of 24. They also have Provost Scholarship valued at $6500 for a GPA of

3.0 on a 4.0 scale, and an SAT of 1000 on the old test, and 1080 on the new test, or ACT of 21 composite. There are non HBCU schools that have school scholarships that are similar, and sometimes the required GPA and or SAT/ACTs are higher, but this example is to inspire you to look for these scholarships to fund your education regardless of your socioeconomic level. These are for students who have the GPA, and test scores.

Texas Southern University has a Regents scholarship with a requirement of 3.75-4.0 GPA, and of 1370+ for the new test and ACT of 30-36 will get max award of $14,000 per year and is renewable for up to three years, and a Presidents scholarship with a requirement of 3.5-3.74 GPA, and SAT of 1240-1369 for the new test, and ACT of 26-29 for a max award of 10,000. These are only the top two awards for these schools, but each school may have up to four or five achievement scholarships that you may be eligible for so you have to look for the money. In addition, this school also has achievement awards for transfer students up to $4000 dollars depending on number of transfer hours, and transfer GPA.

When majoring in science there are often other scholarships like the MARC scholarship to encourage graduate school once you finish your undergraduate degree. There are also scholarships and stipends from the Department of Energy, and the Department of defense that are usually attached to research projects.

Students have gone from HBCU's to Military Academies, Ivy League, and little Ivy League schools, and of course on to professional schools. At the five U.S. Military Academies you have to start over as a freshman, you can transfer to Military Schools/Colleges, and to Ivy League schools except for Princeton. You would have to ask Princeton why. You cannot have been in a major at your other school, or something like that.

You can major in any of the STEM or liberal arts majors, and you can do your entire collegiate journey at the awesome institutions of higher learning. For example, you can go to pharmacy school at to name a few Howard University, FAMU, and Hampton University.

You could do any of your undergraduate degrees at any of the HBCUs, and your MD (not DO yet – maybe at Morgan State University, hopefully at Virginia state University) at Meharry Medical College, Morehouse Medical School, Howard University college of medicine, and Charles Drew school of medicine. Meharry and Howard also have dental schools. You can go to Law school at Howard University, FAMU, North Carolina Central University, Southern University in Louisiana, and Texas Southern University.

These schools also have computer majors, engineering majors, accounting, business, economics, and finance degrees. You can major in just about any area you would like. You may also meet the love of your life at one of these nurturing environments. These schools are also the home to the "Divine Nine" fraternities (Omega Psi Phi is the best), and sororities (Delta Sigma Theta is the best). They are also home or host to other fraternities and sororities.

People continue to come back to these places of learning to enjoy homecoming 30 to 60 years after they graduate. I encourage anyone to look into attending one of these amazing schools regardless of your goals.

Printed in the United States
by Baker & Taylor Publisher Services